MW00737768

Microcomputer Applications

The Benjamin/Cummings Publishing Company, Inc.
Redwood City, California • Menlo Park, California
Reading, Massachusetts • New York • Don Mills, Ontario
Wokingham, U.K. • Amsterdam • Bonn • Sydney
Singapore • Tokyo • Madrid • San Juan

Senior Editor: *Maureen A. Allaire*
Project Editor: *Nancy E. Davis*
Editorial Assistant: *MaryLynne Wrye*
Developmental Editors: *Nancy Canning, Sue Ewing, Rebecca Johnson, Shelly Langman, Evelyn Spire*
Series Editor: *George Beekman*
Executive Editor; B & E, CIS, MIS: *Michael Payne*
Production Manager: *Adam Ray*
Associate Photo Editor: *Lisa Lougee*
Associate Production Editor (Supplements): *Teresa Thomas*
Marketing Manager: *Melissa Baumwald*
Custom Publishing Operations Specialist: *Michael Smith*
Senior Promotions Specialist: *Liane Shayer*
Senior Manufacturing Coordinator: *Janet Weaver*
Manufacturing Supervisor: *Casimira Kostecki*
V.P. Director of Manufacturing and
    Inventory Management, West: *Diane MacIntosh*
Senior Microsystems Analyst: *Craig Johnson*
Production Technologist: *Ari Davidow*
Cover and Text Designer: *Mark Ong, Side-by-Side Studios*
Composition: *CR Waldman Graphics*
Film, Printing, and Binding: *R.R. Donnelley & Sons*

Copyright © 1996 by the Benjamin/Cummings Publishing Company, Inc.

All rights reserved. No part of this publication may be reproduced, stored in a retrieval system, or transmitted, in any form or by any means, electronic, mechanical, photocopying, recording, or otherwise, without the prior written permission of the publisher. Additional copyright and trademark information can be found at the beginning of each application module. Published simultaneously in Canada.

Ordering from the SELECT System

For more information on ordering and pricing policies for the SELECT System of microcomputer applications texts and their supplements, please contact your Addison-Wesley • Benjamin/Cummings sales representative or call our SELECT Hotline at 800/854-2595.

The Benjamin/Cummings Publishing Company, Inc.
390 Bridge Parkway
Redwood City, California 94065

Getting Started

Not too long ago computers were large, impersonal machines hidden away in glass-enclosed, climate-controlled rooms. To use one, you had to either prepare a deck of punched cards and hand them to a professional operator or type cryptic commands, line by line, on a terminal. Today, computers are as accessible and personal as you want them to be. So is the SELECT System.

The SELECT System allows your instructor to customize a group of modules on popular software packages, operating systems, and programming languages for you to learn. The modules themselves are organized around projects that reflect your world and how you will use computers. These projects help you master key concepts and problem-solving techniques while creating documents based on a mix of academic, business, and real-life situations. In the SELECT System, you will apply your computer knowledge in a variety of contexts, just as you will when you leave the classroom.

A GUIDED TOUR

To facilitate the learning process, we have developed a consistent organizational structure for these modules.

You begin using the software almost immediately. A brief *Overview* introduces the software package and the basic application functions. *Getting Help* covers the on-line Help feature in each package. *A Note to the Student* explains any special conventions observed in a particular module.

Each module contains six to eight *Projects*, an *Operations Reference* of commands covered in the module, an extensive *Glossary* of key terms, and an *Index*.

The following figures introduce the elements that you will encounter as you use a SELECT module.

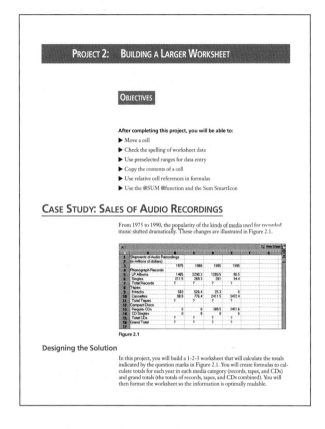

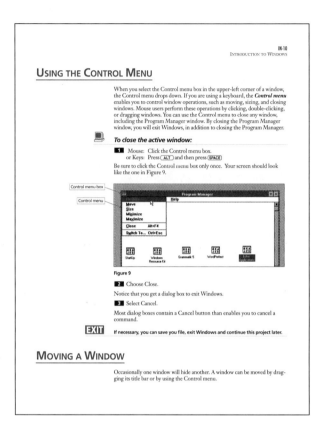

■ Each project begins with *Learning Objectives* that describe the skills and commands you will master.

■ Projects revolve around *Case Studies,* real-world scenarios that allow you to learn an application in a broader context. Case studies give you a sense of when, how, and where an application can serve as an effective tool.

■ *Designing the Solution* introduces you to important problem-solving techniques. You will see how to analyze the case study and design a solution before you sit down at the computer. Thinking through the problem before working with the application allows you to identify the larger issues that must be resolved in order to successfully complete the project.

■ Each topic begins with a brief explanation of concepts you will learn and the operations you will perform.

■ The computer icon provides a cue that you should begin working at the computer. *Numbered steps* guide you step-by-step through each project, providing detailed instructions on how to perform operations. Instructions are provided for both mouse and keyboard where appropriate.

■ Visual cues such as *screen shots* reinforce key concepts and help you check your work. Screen shots provide examples of what you will see on your own computer screen.

■ *Exit points* identify good places in each project to take a break.

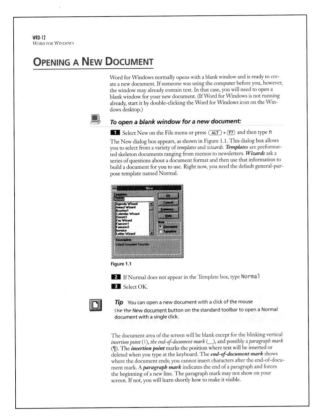

OPENING A NEW DOCUMENT

Word for Windows normally opens with a blank window and is ready to create a new document. If someone was using the computer before you, however, the window may already contain text. In that case, you will need to open a blank window for your new document. (If Word for Windows is not running already, start it by double-clicking the Word for Windows icon on the Windows desktop.)

To open a blank window for a new document:

1. Select New on the File menu or press ALT + F7 and then type n

The New dialog box appears, as shown in Figure 1.1. This dialog box allows you to select from a variety of *templates* and *wizards*. **Templates** are preformatted skeleton documents ranging from memos to newsletters. **Wizards** ask a series of questions about a document format and then use that information to build a document for you to use. Right now, you need the default general-purpose template named Normal.

Figure 1.1

2. If Normal does not appear in the Template box, type Normal
3. Select OK.

Tip You can open a new document with a click of the mouse Use the New document button on the standard toolbar to open a Normal document with a single click.

The document area of the screen will be blank except for the blinking vertical *insertion point* (|), *the end-of-document mark* (___), and possibly a *paragraph mark* (¶). The **insertion point** marks the position where text will be inserted or deleted when you type at the keyboard. The **end-of-document mark** shows where the document ends; you cannot insert characters after the end-of-document mark. A **paragraph mark** indicates the end of a paragraph and forces the beginning of a new line. The paragraph mark may not show on your screen. If not, you will learn shortly how to make it visible.

THE NEXT STEP

Access has many functions that are part of the Access Basic language. You've already seen the Now() function in several reports in this project. If you're interested in extending your knowledge of this aspect of Access, a good place to start is the manual.

There are several other Report Wizards we didn't explore at all. Summary reports have no Detail band. Tabular reports look very much like tabular forms. The AutoReport Wizard will attempt to show your data in the way that makes the most sense—at least, to the Wizard. The final Wizard, MS Word Mail Merge, exports data in a format that Microsoft Word's Mail Merge feature can read. This is handy for producing customized form letters. Experiment with fonts and print styles, an area in which Access excels.

SUMMARY AND EXERCISES

Summary

- Access includes ReportWizards for single-column, grouped, and tabular formats, as well as mailing labels. Wizards are also included that generate automatic reports and export data to Microsoft Word's Mail Merge format
- To build a report with fields from two or more tables, you can query by example to create a view first, and then create the report based on that view.
- Grouping lets you create reports with records collated according to the values in one or more fields.
- Grouping also lets you create subtotals for groups as well as a grand total for the report.
- You can display today's date with the Now() function.
- You can change the format in which the date is printed.
- The mailing label ReportWizard handles standard Avery label layouts.
- To insert text characters in a mailing label, you must use the text buttons provided by the ReportWizards.
- The UCase() function is helpful when you want to make sure report output is entirely upper case.

Key Terms and Operations

Key Terms	
group	report footer
group footer	report header
group header	UCase()
inner join	**Operations**
Now()	Create a new report
outer join	Page Preview
page footer	Report Design
page header	Sample Preview

- **Margin figures** introduce tools from the computer interface. These tools are often convenient alternatives to the menu commands presented in the numbered steps.

- **Tips, Reminders, Cautions,** and **Quick Fixes** appear throughout each project to highlight important, helpful, or pertinent information about each application. This extra level of support clearly identifies useful reference material and helps you work independently.

- **Key Terms** are boldfaced and italicized and appear throughout the module.

- Each project ends with **The Next Step,** a **Summary** of concepts covered in the project, and a list of **Key Terms and Operations.** The Next Step discusses the concepts from the project and proposes other uses and applications for the skills you have learned.

- At the end of each project, you'll find **Study Questions** (multiple-choice, short answer, and discussion), which may be used as a self-test or as a homework assignment.

- **Review Exercises** present hands-on tasks with abbreviated instructions to help you build on skills acquired in the project.

- **Assignments** draw on skills that have been introduced in the project. They encourage you to synthesize and integrate what you have learned through problems that require analysis and critical thinking to complete.

FOLLOWING THE NUMBERED STEPS

To make the application modules easy to use in a lab setting, we have standardized the presentation of hands-on computer instructions as much as possible. The numbered step sections provide detailed, step-by-step instructions to guide you through the practical application of the conceptual material presented. Both keystroke and mouse instructions are used according to which is more appropriate to complete a task. The instructions in the module assume that you know how to operate the keyboard, monitor, and printer.

> **Tip** When you are using a mouse, unless indicated otherwise, you should assume that you are clicking the left button on the mouse. Several modules provide instructions for both mouse and keyboard users. When separate mouse and keyboard steps are given, be sure to follow one method or the other, but not both.

Each topic begins with a brief explanation of concepts. A computer icon or the ▶ symbol and a description of the task you will perform appear each time you are to begin working on the computer.

For Example:

To enter the address:

1 Type `123 Elm Street` and press `(ENTER)`

Notice that the keys you will press and the text you will type stand out. The text you will type appears in a special typface to distinguish it from regular text. The key you will press mimics the labels of the keys on your keyboard.

When you need to press two keys or a key and a character simultaneously, the steps show the keys connected either with a plus sign or a bar.

For Example:

`(SHFT)` + `(TAB)`
`(CTRL)` + C

When you need to press keys sequentially, the keys are not connected and a space separates them.

For Example:

`(CTRL)` `(PGDN)`
`(HOME)` `(HOME)` `(↑)`

Be sure to press each key firmly, but quickly, one after the other. Keys begin repeating if you hold them down too long.

In some instances margin figures of single icons or buttons will appear next to the numbered steps. Margin figures provide visual cues to important tools that you can select as an alternative to the menu command in the numbered step.

For typographical conventions and other information unique to the application, please see *A Note to the Student* in the Overview of each module.

AN OVERVIEW OF THE **SELECT** SERIES

Your instructor can choose any combination of concepts texts and applications modules listed below, and we bind them into one convenient, affordable text.

Concepts Texts

Computers and Information Systems, Fourth Edition, by H.L. Capron

Essentials of Computing, Second Edition, by H.L. Capron

Computer Currents: Navigating Tomorrow's Technology, by George Beekman

Computers in Context: Using Microcomputer Applications, by Carl A. Scharpf

Applications Modules

Each SELECT Edition that covers a Windows-based application includes a complimentary *Introduction to Windows* section.

Windows	DOS
Word Processing	
WordPerfect 6.1 Projects for Windows	WordPerfect 6.0 Projects for DOS
WordPerfect 6 Projects for Windows	Projects for WordPerfect 5.1
WordPerfect 5.2 Projects for Windows	
Microsoft Word 6 Projects for Windows	
Spreadsheets	
Lotus 1-2-3 Rel. 4 Projects for Windows	Projects for Lotus 1-2-3, Rel. 2.3/2.4
Microsoft Excel 5 Projects for Windows	Projects for Lotus 1-2-3, Rel. 2.2
Microsoft Excel 4.0 Projects for Windows	Projects for Quattro Pro 4.0/5.0
Projects for Excel 3.0 (PC Version)	
Quattro Pro 6 Projects for Windows	
Quattro Pro 1.0/5.0 Projects for Windows	
Database	
Microsoft Access 2 Projects for Windows	Projects for dBASE IV
Paradox 5 Projects for Windows	Projects for dBASE III PLUS
Paradox Projects for Windows	Projects for Paradox 3.5
Presentation Graphics Packages	
Microsoft PowerPoint 4 Projects for Windows	
Integrated Packages	
Microsoft Works 3 Projects for Windows	Projects for Microsoft Works 3.0
	Projects for Microsoft Works 2.0

DOS/Windows Applications Modules

Projects for Windows 95
Projects for DOS 6.0 and Windows 3.1
Projects for DOS 5.0 and Windows 3.1
Projects for DOS 2.0/3.3 and Windows 3.0

Programming Modules

Microsoft Visual Basic 3.0 Projects for Windows	Structured Basic for Beginners
	QBasic for Beginners

ACKNOWLEDGMENTS

The Benjamin/Cummings Publishing Company would like to thank George Beekman for his valuable contributions as the SELECT Series Editor. Equally important are the contributions of our reviewers:

Joseph Aieta
Babson College

Roger Anderson
College of Lake County

Tom Ashby
Oklahoma City CC

Bob Barber
Lane CC

Ronald Burgher
Metropolitan CC

Terry Byrd
Auburn University

Robert Caruso
Santa Rosa Junior College

Paul Chase
Becker College

Robert Chi
California State
 University, Long Beach

Robert Clark
Buffalo State College

Martin Crossland
Southwest Missouri
 State University

Jill Davis
State University of
 New York at Stony Brook

Fredia Dillard
Samford University

Peter Drexel
Plymouth State College

Ralph Duffy
North Seattle CC

David Egle
University of Texas,
 Pan American

Raymond Folse
Nicholls State University

Jonathan Frank
Suffolk University

Patrick Gilbert
University of Hawaii

Maureen Greenbaum
Union County College

Sally Ann Hanson
Mercer County CC

Sunil Hazari
East Carolina University

Bruce Herniter
University of Hartford

Lisa Jackson
Henderson CC

Cynthia Kachik
Santa Fe CC

Harold Kollmeier
Franklin Pierce College

Bennett Kramer
Massasoit CC

Charles Lake
Faulkner State
 Junior College

Ron Leake
Johnson County CC

Dennis Lynch
Elgin CC

Randy Marak
Hill College

Charles Mattox Jr.
St. Mary's University

Jim McCullough
Porter and Chester
 Institute

Vickie McCullough
Palomar College

Gail Miles
Lenoir-Rhyne College

Linda Wise Miller
University of Idaho

Lawrence Molloy
Oakland CC

Carolyn Monroe
Baylor University

Steve Moore
University of South
 Florida

Uday Murthy
IUPUI

Anthony Nowakowski
Buffalo State College

Gloria Oman
Portland State University

John Passafiume
Clemson University

Leonard Presby
William Paterson College

Louis Pryor
Garland County CC

Tonia Queen
Brevard CC

Michael Reilly
University of Denver

Dick Ricketts
Lane CC

Dennis Santomauro
Kean College of
 New Jersey

Pamela Schmidt
Oakton CC

Gary Schubert
Alderson-Broaddus
 College

Jennifer Sedelmeyer
Broome CC

Patricia Smith
Temple Junior College

T. Michael Smith
Austin CC

Cynthia Thompson
Carl Sandburg College

Marion Tucker
Northern Oklahoma
 College

JoAnn Weatherwax
Saddleback College

Melinda White
Santa Fe CC

David Whitney
San Francisco State
 University

James Wood
Tri-County Technical
 College

Minnie Yen
University of Alaska,
 Anchorage

Allen Zilbert
Long Island University

SUPPLEMENTS

Each module has a corresponding Instructor's Manual with a Test Bank and Transparency Masters. For each project in the student text, the Instructor's Manual includes Expanded Student Objectives, Answers to Study Questions, and Additional Assessment Techniques. The Test Bank contains two separate tests (with answers) consisting of multiple choice, true/false, and fill-in questions referenced to pages in the student's text. Transparency Masters illustrate 25 to 30 key concepts and screen captures from the text.

The Instructor's Data Disk contains student data files, answers to selected Review Exercises, answers to selected Assignments, and the test files from the Instructor's Manual in ASCII format.

Introduction to Windows

Objectives

In this introduction, you will learn how to:

▶ Use a mouse

▶ Start and exit Windows

▶ Get help in Windows

▶ Access the Program Manager menu and the Control menu

▶ Use a dialog box

▶ Manipulate windows and icons

▶ Start and exit a program

Since the introduction of computers in the 1940s, an evolution has occurred. Operations such as saving, loading, and running a program on early computers required an extraordinary degree of knowledge and the skills of a specialist. After the 1950s, these same tasks were performed by operating systems, groups of programs that control and supervise the computer system operations. Since the introduction of graphical user interfaces in the 1980s, computers work on the user's terms. Even computer novices can quickly learn to use the visual display of these "user friendly" environments.

USING WINDOWS 3.1

An *operating system* is a complex set of instructions that manages a computer's resources. Windows 3.1 is a full-featured graphical operating environment that greatly extends the capabilities of DOS, IBM's disk operating system. Windows is not an operating system, but an operating environment that runs "on top of" DOS. First you load DOS, and then you load Windows. Application programs, such as Microsoft Excel and Microsoft Word, are then loaded under Windows.

The DOS command line is replaced with a ***graphical user interface (GUI)*** that is much easier to learn than DOS's text-based interface. The Windows ***desktop*** (the screen background) serves as a graphical-based work area (see Figure 1). Application programs and documents are found inside different ***windows*** (rectangular areas on the desktop). In a graphical user interface, operations are executed by selecting ***icons,*** graphical representations of Windows elements, and by choosing options from lists of commands called ***menus.*** For example, to copy a disk, you choose the Copy Disk command from the Disk menu.

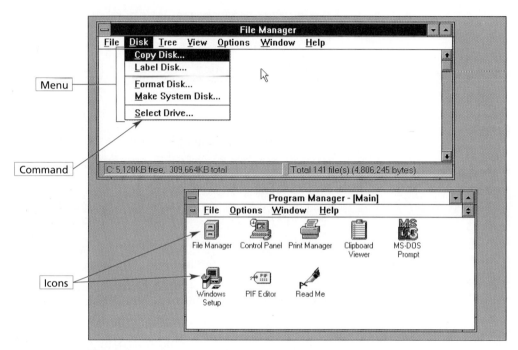

Figure 1

To take full advantage of all of the features in Windows 3.1, you must buy special versions of software programs, known as ***Windows applications.*** When you buy an application software package, the product's box will indicate whether it has been written specifically for Windows. This does not mean that only Windows applications can run under Windows. Almost all programs run under Windows, but ***non-Windows applications,*** programs not designed specifically for Windows, cannot take advantage of many of Windows' features.

A Note to the Student

The instructions in the projects describe how to execute commands with a mouse. Comparable keyboard keystrokes are included for computer systems without a mouse. For example, a typical instruction will look like:

1 Mouse: Click File on the menu bar.
   or Keys: Press (ALT) + F

Refer to the *Getting Started* section for a detailed explanation of how keystrokes are presented in the module.

USING A MOUSE

Windows 3.1 is designed to be used with a pointing device such as a mouse or trackball. A *mouse* is a hand-held input device that is rolled on a small flat surface, usually a table or mouse pad. The movement of the mouse causes a corresponding movement of a pointer on the screen. A *trackball* performs the same function as a mouse but works somewhat differently. You use your fingers to roll a ball that is exposed on the top of the device, which causes the pointer to move on the screen.

There are several common terms that you need to know when using a mouse. The *pointer* is a symbol (usually an arrow) that moves around the screen as you move your mouse. To *click* means to position the pointer on an object and then quickly press and release the left mouse button. A *double-click* involves the same motion as a click, but the mouse button is pressed and released twice in rapid succession. Usually this causes a small hourglass icon to appear on the screen for a few seconds. The hourglass indicates that you need to wait while Windows loads something. When you *drag* an object, you will hold down the left mouse button while moving the mouse. Dragging is used for moving or sizing an object or choosing commands.

The *menu bar* lists available menus. An application usually has File, Edit, and Help menus, in addition to the application's unique menus. To use a mouse to choose a command, you will click the name of the menu on the menu bar. A *drop-down menu,* a menu that drops down onto the screen, will appear, as shown in Figure 2. While holding down the left mouse button, you will highlight the desired command and then release the button to execute the command. Alternatively, you can execute a command by clicking the command in the drop-down menu.

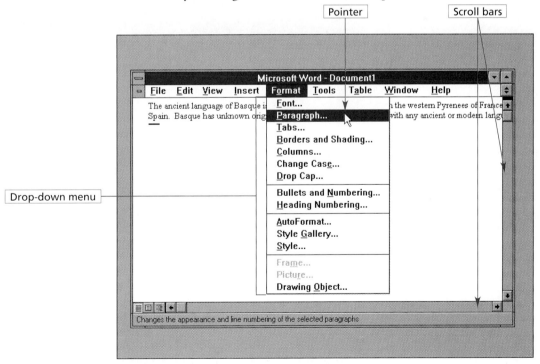

Figure 2

Some windows have bars, called **scroll bars,** along the right and/or bottom border. Figure 2 displays scroll bars for scrolling through a document. You can move through the document or the list of choices one line at a time by clicking either arrow at the end of the scroll bar. You can move to a specific location by dragging the **scroll box,** the box within the scroll bar. You can also scroll with the keyboard one line at a time by pressing ⊙ and ⊙ or one screen at a time by pressing (PGUP) and (PGDN).

STARTING AND EXITING WINDOWS

The following steps describe the standard method for starting Windows. Before you can begin, DOS must be installed in the computer. But since DOS is typically installed with hard disk and networked systems, you only need to turn on the computer's power.

How you start Windows itself depends on how your computer is set up. For example, your computer may be running a menu system or the DOS Shell that facilitates the starting of Windows. A typical setup is for a computer screen to display the DOS prompt, which is a letter followed by a > sign. A> and B> are used for floppy disk systems, C> for hard disk systems, and F> for network systems.

To start Windows:

1 Type **win** at the DOS prompt and press (ENTER)
The first screen to appear is the Windows 3.1 logo, which is soon followed by a window called the Program Manager. Your screen may look a little different from the one in Figure 3.

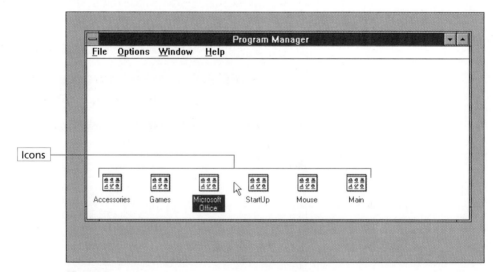

Icons

Figure 3

To exit Windows:

1 Mouse: Click File on the menu bar.
   or Keys: Press (ALT)+F
Your screen should look like the one in Figure 4.

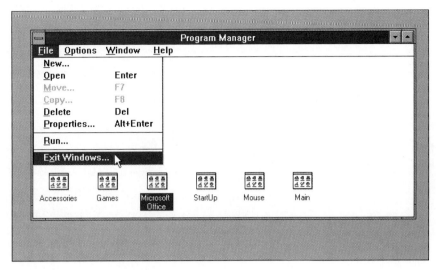

Figure 4

2 Mouse: Click Exit Windows.
   or Keys: Press **X**

3 Mouse: Click OK.
   or Keys: Press (ENTER)

GETTING HELP

The Help menu within the Program Manager provides assistance for the Program Manager and for most Windows concepts, commands, and terms. You access Help by choosing the Help command from the menu system. If you are in the process of executing a command, press (F1) for help.

To access Help, and then access the Help Contents:

1 Make sure you are in Windows.

2 Mouse: Click Help.
   or Keys: Press (ALT)+**H**

3 Mouse: Click Contents.
   or Keys: Press **C**

Your screen should look like Figure 5.

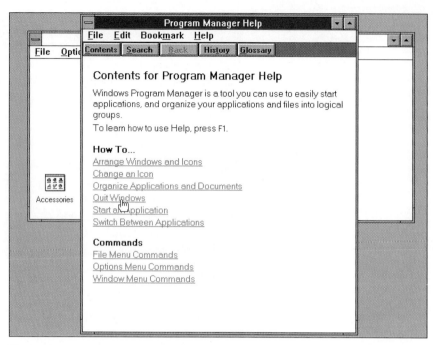

Figure 5

The Contents command, which displays the topics for the Program Manager Help, is a good place to begin exploring Help.

To get help quitting Windows:

1 Mouse: Click Quit Windows under the How To heading.

   or Keys: Press (TAB) until you highlight Quit Windows, and then press (ENTER)

You should see a description of how to exit Windows, as shown in Figure 6.

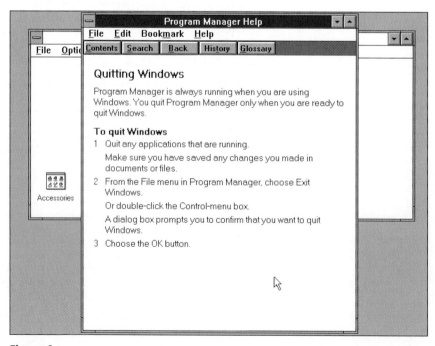

Figure 6

Figure 6 displays five buttons, common to all Help screens, that you can access by clicking or pressing (ALT) and the corresponding underlined letter. The Contents button displays the topics for the Program Manager Help, Search enables you to type keywords to look up Help information, Back takes you back to a previous Help screen, History lists the names of the Help screens that you have displayed, and Glossary provides a list of definitions for important words.

To go back to the previous Help screen:

1 Mouse: Click the Back button.
or Keys: Press (ALT) + **B**

Your screen should display the Contents for the Program Manager Help screen. Notice that the Back button is dimmed to indicate that you cannot go back to any other Help screens; that is, this is the screen from which you started.

The Search button enables you to type in a keyword and then have Windows search for any information related to it.

To search for Help on starting an application:

1 Mouse: Click the Search button.
or Keys: Press (ALT) + **S**

2 Type **starting** and then press (ENTER)

The search screen should display five topics that are found under *starting applications*, as shown in Figure 7.

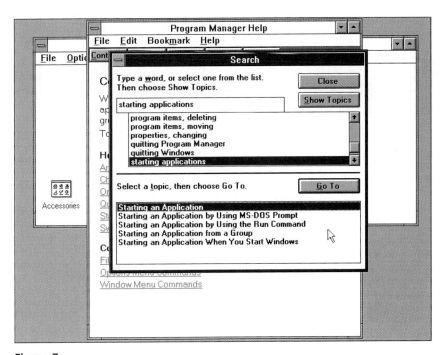

Figure 7

3 Mouse: Double-click Starting an Application from a Group.
or Keys: Press (⬇) until you highlight Starting an Application from a Group, and then press (ENTER)

Your screen should display the Starting an Application from a Group Help screen.

To look up a word in the Glossary:

1 Mouse: Click *group*
or Keys: Press TAB until *group* is highlighted, and then press ENTER

2 Press ESC to return to the previous window.

An alternative method for looking up the definition of a word is by clicking the Glossary button for a complete list of all of Windows' glossary items.

> **Tip** Now that you have seen how to access menu commands and screen buttons using either the mouse or the keyboard, you can use the method or combination of methods you prefer. From now on, the instructions will be stated in more general terms and will look like this:
>   Choose Contents   *or*   Select Search
> The word *choose* refers to menu commands, and the word *select* refers to options (such as the Help buttons).

To exit Help:

1 Choose Exit from the File Menu.

If you access Help from within a software application, you will receive help on that particular application. The Help feature will work in the same fashion, but the command options and the Help screens will pertain to the application. In many applications, Help will be context-sensitive. For example, if you are in the process of saving a document in Microsoft Word and you press F1, you will get help on saving a document in Word and avoid searching through the Help screens to find the right screen.

USING THE PROGRAM MANAGER MENU

The ***Program Manager*** performs a pivotal role in the operation of Windows. It automatically opens every time you start Windows and remains in the background during your entire Windows session. When you are ready to quit Windows, you do so by closing the Program Manager. The Program Manager gives you a quick and easy way to start applications.

To display the Program Manager:

1 If you have not done so already, start Windows.

Figure 8 shows a typical Program Manager window. The names and the arrangement of the program group icons on your screen may be different.

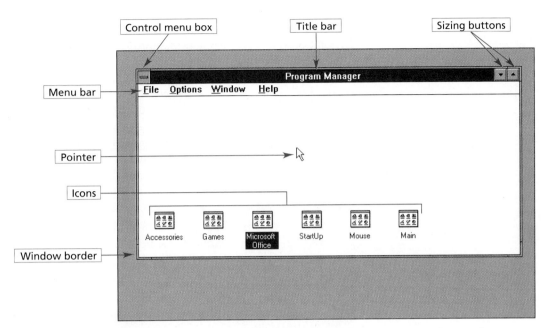

Figure 8

Each window has a ***Control menu box*** in its upper-left corner from which a drop-down menu appears that lists commands for controlling a window. With a mouse, you can use the ***sizing buttons*** to change the dimensions of the window quickly. The name of the application or document is displayed in the ***title bar.*** The ***window border*** defines the outside edge of the window.

Within Windows, you perform many operations by choosing menu options. The Program Manager's menus provide basic commands for managing windows and applications. For example, you can open, copy, and delete applications. You also can get help on the Program Manager and on other parts of Windows. When you select a menu from the menu bar, the menus that drop down follow three conventions that are common among most Windows menus: checkmarks, dimmed commands, and ellipses. A ***checkmark*** next to a command name indicates that a command is active. Only optional commands that can be ***toggled*** (turned on and off) are displayed with checkmarks.

A ***dimmed command*** on a menu is not available at the current time. Some commands are available only during certain situations; when they are dimmed, they cannot be executed.

An ***ellipsis,*** the three-dot symbol (...) that follows certain commands, denotes that a dialog box will appear when the command is chosen. A ***dialog box*** is a rectangular box that either prompts the user to provide more information or provides information of its own, such as a warning or error message.

USING THE CONTROL MENU

When you select the Control menu box in the upper-left corner of a window, the Control menu drops down. If you are using a keyboard, the *Control menu* enables you to control window operations, such as moving, sizing, and closing windows. Mouse users perform these operations by clicking, double-clicking, or dragging windows. You can use the Control menu to close any window, including the Program Manager window. By closing the Program Manager window, you will exit Windows, in addition to closing the Program Manager.

To close the active window:

1 Mouse: Click the Control menu box.
   or Keys: Press (ALT) and then press (SPACE)
Be sure to click the Control menu box only once. Your screen should look like the one in Figure 9.

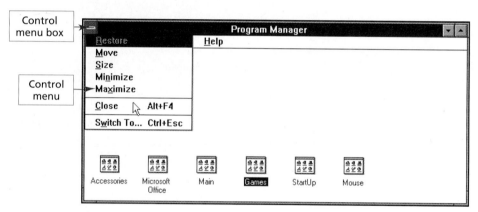

Figure 9

2 Choose Close.
Notice that you get a dialog box to exit Windows.

3 Select Cancel.
Most dialog boxes contain a Cancel button that enables you to cancel a command.

MOVING A WINDOW

Occasionally one window will hide another. A window can be moved by dragging its title bar or by using the Control menu.

To move the Program Manager window:

1 Mouse: Place the pointer anywhere on the Program Manager title bar.
   or Keys: Press (ALT) + (SPACE)

■2 Mouse: Click the title bar and hold down the mouse button.
  or Keys: Press **M**

■3 Mouse: Drag the pointer a little to the right.
  or Keys: Press ⊙ a few times.

■4 Mouse: Release the mouse button.
  or Keys: Press (ENTER)

■5 Move the Program Manager window back to its original position.

SIZING A WINDOW

Sizing a window requires a steady hand. You will move the pointer to the edge of the window until the pointer's shape changes, and then drag the edges.

> **Tip** Do not click the mouse in these operations until the pointer changes into the appropriate shape.
> ↔ Changes the width of a window
> ↕ Changes the height of a window
> ↘ Changes the height and width of a window simultaneously

To increase the height of a window:

■1 Mouse: Place the pointer on the upper border of the window until the pointer becomes double-pointed.
  or Keys: Press (ALT)+(SPACE) and then press **S**

■2 Mouse: Drag the pointer upward a short distance, and then release the mouse button.
  or Keys: Press ⊙ once to place the pointer on the upper border. Press ⊙ a few times to move the upper border and then press (ENTER)

You can also change the height of a window by dragging the lower border up or down.

To increase the width of a window:

■1 Mouse: Place the pointer on the right side of the window border until the pointer becomes double-pointed.
  or Keys: Press (ALT)+(SPACE) and then press **S**

■2 Mouse: Drag the pointer a short distance to the right, and then let go of the mouse button.
  or Keys: Press ⊙ once to place the pointer on the right border. Press ⊙ a few times and then press (ENTER)

You can also change a window's width by dragging its left border left or right.

To simultaneously change the height and width of a window:

■1 Mouse: Place the pointer in the lower-right corner of the window until the pointer becomes diagonal and double-pointed.
  or Keys: Press (ALT)+(SPACE) and then press **S**
            Press ⊙ once, and then press ⊙ once.

2 Mouse: Drag the pointer a short distance upward and to the left.

or Keys: Press ⬆ and ⬅ a few times and then press (ENTER)

MANIPULATING WINDOWS

To concentrate all of your attention on one particular window, you can use the Windows Minimize and Maximize buttons shown in Figure 10. To *maximize* a window means to fill the entire screen with the window.

Figure 10

To maximize a window:

1 Mouse: Click the Maximize button.

or Keys: Press (ALT) + (SPACE) and then press **X**

The Program Manager window should fill the entire screen.

To *restore* a window means to bring it back to its previous size. The Restore button is shown in Figure 11.

Figure 11

To restore a window after it has been maximized:

1 Mouse: Click the Restore button.

or Keys: Press (ALT) + (SPACE) and then press **R**

To *minimize* a window means to reduce it to an icon at the bottom of the screen. The application can be easily restored later to its former size by double-clicking the icon. An icon can be identified by its distinct shape or its name, which always appears below the icon.

To minimize and then restore the Program Manager:

1 Mouse: Click the Minimize button.

or Keys: Press (ALT) + (SPACE) and then press **N**

The minimized Program Manager will be displayed as an icon.

2 Mouse: Double-click the Program Manager icon.

or Keys: Press (ALT) + (SPACE) and then press **R**

Tip If you are using the keyboard and have multiple application icons on the screen, you will need to press (ALT) + (ESC) to select the Program Manager icon before you can restore the Program Manager.

WORKING WITH ICONS

Figure 12 shows Windows' three basic types of icons: application icons, group icons, and program-item icons.

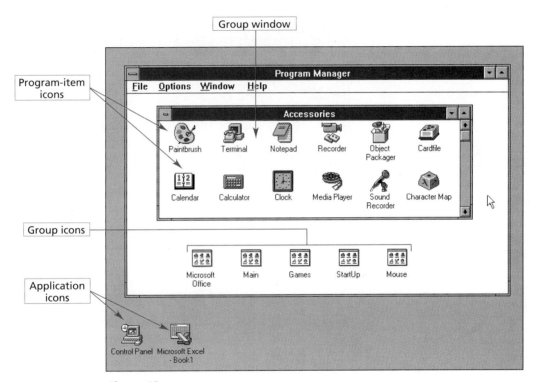

Figure 12

An ***application icon*** represents a program that has been minimized. In the Program Manager, ***group icons*** represent groups of programs. Group icons open into ***group windows*** filled with programs. In general, group icons look the same except for their labels.

A ***program-item icon*** is used to start an application. When you open a program-item icon, a window opens with the program inside. The Accessories group in Figure 12 contains program-item icons for programs such as the Clock, the Calculator, and the Calendar. If you were to open the Windows Applications group icon in Figure 12, you would see the Word and Excel program-item icons in the group window. Word and Excel's program-item icons look the same as their application icons.

STARTING A PROGRAM

One of the Program Manager's main roles is to start programs (lists of instructions). When you start a program, the Program Manager opens a window and places the program into it. Programs and their associated documents are contained in application and document windows.

An **application window** contains a running **application**, a program designed for a particular type of work. For example, the Program Manager runs in an application window as does a word processing program such as Microsoft Word. Figure 13 displays a Microsoft Word application window.

Application window
Document window

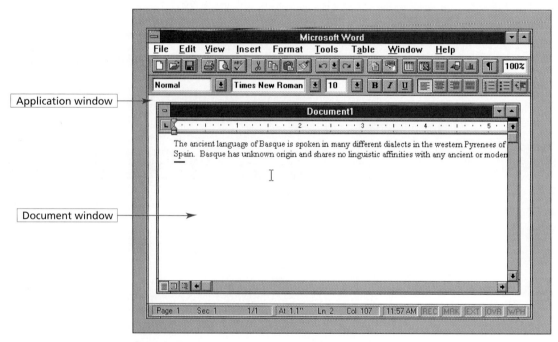

Figure 13

A **document window** is found inside of an application window and contains a **document**, such as a letter, memo, or report. If you are working on multiple documents simultaneously, you will have multiple document windows open.

The Program Manager uses group windows, such as the Accessories group window, which are similar to document windows because they reside within an application window.

To open the Accessories group window:

1 Choose Options.

2 Mouse: Make sure Minimize On Use is *not* checked. If it is not checked, click the desktop. If it is checked, click Minimize On Use to toggle it on.

or Keys: If Minimize On Use is *not* checked, press (ESC) twice; otherwise, press **M**

When Minimize On Use is checked, the Program Manager will minimize itself every time that you open an application. In this introduction, we don't want that to happen.

3 Mouse: Double-click the Accessories group icon to open Accessories.

or Keys: Press (CTRL)+(F6) until the Accessories group icon is highlighted, and then press (ENTER)

The Accessories group includes utility programs that are provided as part of the Windows software package. For example, the *Calendar* serves as an electronic appointment book with an alarm to remind you of important appointments.

To open the Calendar program:

Calendar

1 Mouse: Double-click the Calendar program-item icon. If necessary, scroll through Accessories to find the Calendar.

or Keys: Press the arrow keys until the Calendar is highlighted. Press (ENTER)

Your screen should look like the one in Figure 14. Your Calendar may be positioned differently.

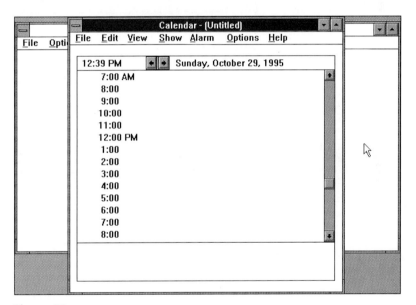

Figure 14

SETTING DIALOG BOX OPTIONS

Dialog boxes display information and prompt you to enter text. You can also adjust the settings of Windows options by using option buttons, command buttons, and check boxes. You move the cursor from one option to another by clicking the option or pressing (TAB).

Option buttons appear in small groups of related options from which you can select only one item.

To set printer options:

1 Choose Print Setup from the File menu.
In the box labeled Orientation, you can choose one of two option buttons, Portrait or Landscape, as shown in Figure 15. A portrait orientation prints the document vertically on the paper; a landscape orientation prints horizontally.

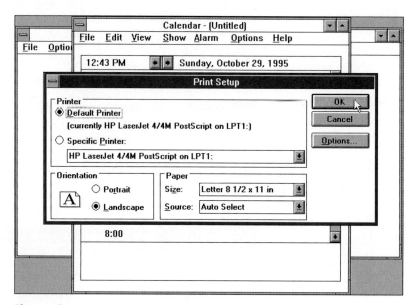

Figure 15

2 Select Landscape.

Command buttons are rectangular buttons labeled with an action. Figure 15 contains the two most common command buttons, OK and Cancel, and the Options command button.

To close a dialog box without saving any new settings:

1 Select Cancel.

EXITING PROGRAMS

You can close most programs in Windows by choosing the Exit command from the File menu.

To exit the Calendar:

1 Choose Exit from the File menu.

To restore the Program Manager and exit Windows:

1 Restore the Program Manager.

2 Use one of the methods that you have learned to exit Windows.

This concludes your introduction to Windows.

Microsoft Visual Basic 3.0 Projects for Windows

Paul B. Thurrott

Gary R. Brent
Scottsdale Community College

James R. Elam
Scottsdale Community College

The Benjamin/Cummings Publishing Company, Inc.
Redwood City, California • Menlo Park, California
Reading, Massachusetts • New York • Don Mills, Ontario
Wokingham, U.K. • Amsterdam • Bonn • Sydney
Singapore • Tokyo • Madrid • San Juan

ISBN 0-8053-1187-4

Copyright © 1996 by the Benjamin/Cummings Publishing Company, Inc.

Microsoft, Visual Basic, and Windows are registered trademarks of Microsoft Corporation.

All rights reserved. No part of this publication may be reproduced, stored in a database or retrieval system, distributed or transmitted, in any form or by any means, electronic, mechanical, photocopying, recording, or otherwise, without the prior written permission of the publisher. Printed in the United States of America. Published simultaneously in Canada.

To Stephanie —PBT

To my children—GRB

To Lisa and Stella Louise—JRE

Contents

Overview

Objectives

After completing this Overview, you should be able to:

▶ List the steps needed to create a Visual Basic program

▶ Define syntax and logic errors

▶ Start Visual Basic version 3.0

▶ Identify key areas of the Visual Basic interface

▶ Access Visual Basic Help

▶ Exit Visual Basic

What makes computer software different from other kinds of modern technology? Perhaps the most unusual aspect of software is that it is intangible: It is not a physical entity at all. It is, rather, like an abstract machine whose cogs and gears are objects of the imagination. It has been said that without software, computer hardware is not very functional or interesting. It is software that enables you to use your computer to simulate flight, play games, compute financial analyses, paint pictures, and communicate with people on the far side of the globe. Though software would be equally useless without hardware, it is ultimately the software that creates the real magic in a personal computer and makes it a universal machine.

Perhaps to this point you have been primarily a *user* of software: someone who employs programs written by others. In this module you will learn to create your own Windows programs using the Visual Basic programming language. You are in an enviable position. As recently as the late 1980s, programmers wanting to learn Windows programming faced an unmanageable mountain of software development tools, the difficult C language, and a partially undocumented interface. Today, with Visual

Basic, you can create Windows programs with an ease that was impossible only a few years ago.

It is time to create some magic of your own.

CREATING COMPUTER PROGRAMS

A computer *program* is a series of instructions that causes the computer to perform certain tasks. When the computer carries out the instructions in a program, it is said to *run* or *execute* the program. The computer can only execute instructions written in its native *machine language* or *machine code,* which consists essentially of numerical codes for each operation. Programs are written by people called *programmers.* It is extremely difficult and time-consuming for programmers to write their programs in machine code, because machine code is so unlike human language. Instead, a programmer can use a *programming language,* which is much easier to understand than machine code.

There are dozens of different programming languages, each with its own vocabulary and grammar rules. Some programming languages are easier for people to learn than others, in the same way that Spanish is easier for most people to learn than Sanskrit or Classical Chinese. Sometimes groups of programming languages are related to one another, making it easier to learn one if you know another, in the same way that knowing one Romance language, such as Italian, makes it easier to learn another related language, such as French, Spanish, or Portuguese.

A human-readable program, written by a programmer in a specific programming language, is called *source code.* Unfortunately, the computer cannot understand source code, so a translation program must be used to change source code into computer-readable machine code. There are two major types of tools that perform this translation: interpreters and compilers.

An *interpreter* translates the source code program line-by-line as the program is executed, in the same way that a human interpreter translates words spoken in a foreign language as they are spoken. Because this translation occurs as the program is running, interpreted languages usually run rather slowly. Interpreted languages do, however, allow programs to be *partially executed:* A program that is incomplete can still be run, although it may end prematurely. Historically, most versions of BASIC have been interpreted.

A *compiler* translates the source code all at once, generating a separate executable machine code file that can be directly understood and run by the computer. Compilers are like people who translate books into a new language: The book can then be read all at once, without the reader having to wait for the translator. Compiled code runs faster than interpreted code but does not offer the benefits of immediate testing and partial execution.

Visual Basic is a curious cross between traditional interpreted BASICs of the past and compiled languages. Visual Basic programs can be compiled into *p-code,* or *packed code,* so named because it stores information in a far more efficient manner than normal source code is stored. This p-code is then interpreted as the program runs. P-code is in a partially translated form that is more compact but slower than true machine code. Though the p-code that Visual Basic generates will run faster than traditional interpreted languages, it is still slower than a true compiled language.

A SHORT HISTORY OF **BASIC**

The programming language BASIC (an acronym for Beginner's All-Purpose Symbolic Instruction Code) was created in the early 1960s by John Kemeny and Thomas Kurtz at Dartmouth College. Unlike the rather arcane computer languages that preceded it, BASIC was designed for non-programmers, and it uses English-like source code that is easy to read and understand. Early versions of BASIC were interpreted because of the small memory sizes of the computers that were then available.

Microsoft, the company responsible for DOS, Windows, Word, Excel, and other popular desktop software, has its roots in BASIC. Microsoft's first product was a BASIC interpreter for the MITS Altair, the first microcomputer. Over the years, Microsoft has improved BASIC, releasing GW-BASIC, QBasic, and QuickBasic for IBM-compatible personal computers.

The rise in popularity of Windows led Microsoft to develop Visual Basic. Windows applications are well known for being hard to create, with a bewildering array of concepts to learn. Visual Basic takes the complexity out of Windows programming and adds the element it has so sadly lacked—fun. Visual Basic programming is quick, easy, and surprisingly powerful. It also provides *code compatibility* with QuickBasic and QBasic: Source code developed for those DOS-based languages is easily converted to Visual Basic.

The initial release of Visual Basic for Windows was an overnight success, and Microsoft has since released two major updates, including version 3.0 in 1993. Each release has added to the strength of the product, improving performance and adding features. As a result, Visual Basic is a mature and stable product.

You may have noticed that there are two separate editions of Visual Basic 3.0: the Standard Edition and the Professional Edition. Both editions are fully code-compatible with each other. Either version may be used to successfully complete the projects in this book. Figure 0.1 shows the Standard Edition. The Professional Edition, shown in Figure 0.2, offers some enhancements to the Standard Edition, such as a larger collection of built-in controls. The projects and figures in this book were generated using the Standard Edition.

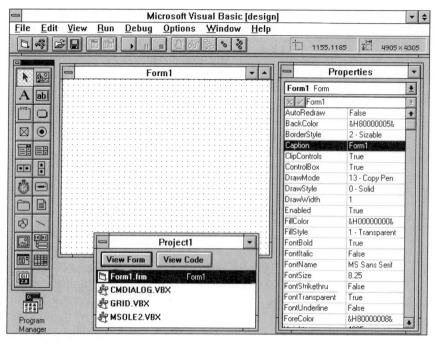

Figure 0.1

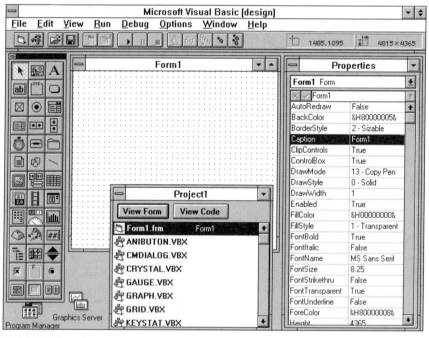

Figure 0.2

A Note to the Student

This module assumes the following:

- Visual Basic is installed on the hard disk of the computer you will be using.

- You will store all the Visual Basic program files you create in the root directory of a diskette in drive A. If you are using another drive and/or directory, you will need to substitute it for drive A in the appropriate steps in the text.
- Your diskette, and a backup diskette, are formatted and ready to use.
- You are familiar with Windows. If not, please review the *Introduction to Windows* in the beginning of this book.

VISUAL BASIC CONCEPTS

Visual Basic is very different from other Windows programming languages and applications. As such, it may be confusing at first to the new user. Don't worry! Visual Basic is easy to use, but as with any new program, there are a few concepts that you will need to be acquainted with. For example, Visual Basic looks at Windows in a unique way.

Event-Driven Programming

The earliest computer programs did not interact with the user at all: The program would be loaded into the computer, perhaps from a deck of punched cards, and would run to completion, usually producing its final results on a paper printout. As the capabilities of computers improved, programs became more interactive: The user might, for example, use a terminal to respond to a series of prompts or use a menu system.

Most contemporary programs are highly interactive. A Windows program must respond to the user's mouse clicks, menu selections, button presses, and many other events. These events, and a program's ability to respond to them, form the basis of *event-driven programming*. Sections of code are executed only when an event triggers them. With Visual Basic, an event-driven program is, for the first time, easy to write and understand.

In Visual Basic, programs are created using a building-block approach, starting with a blank window called a *form*. Each element, or *object*, in a Visual Basic program is definable by the programmer. Objects like command buttons, menus, and text boxes are *placed* directly on the form to create the user interface for your program. *Controls*, as these objects are known, provide the "look and feel" of your program: the visual front end with which the user will interact.

Each control has *properties*, or attributes, that the Visual Basic programmer can easily change. These properties allow you to customize each of the objects in your program.

Deciding how your program interacts with the user involves deciding which events each control should respond to. It is like connecting wires to the various controls on an instrument panel. You decide how the internal components of your program will be connected to and triggered by actions that happen to the controls on the visible form.

DESIGNING A VISUAL BASIC APPLICATION

It is always a good idea to plan ahead when beginning any programming project. The following steps are designed to allow the planning and building of a Visual Basic program to proceed in a logical fashion.

1. **Identify the specification.** You must be clear about what the program is supposed to do. The specification, written in simple English, can be as short as a few sentences or can stretch to many pages, depending on the complexity of the problem. Think of the specification as a precise statement by the user, describing what the program should do.

2. **Sketch the interface.** Make a rough sketch of what the forms and controls in your program will look like. List the various properties of each object in your program. You can then refer to this sketch when you actually sit down at the keyboard and type.

3. **Decide which events you want to trigger program actions.** For each object, whether a form or a control, you should identify the events you want that object to respond to. For example, a command button labeled *Quit* should end the program.

4. **Draw a flowchart that shows the relationship between major objects, events, and actions.** Use brief descriptions of actions that should occur in response to events. This module uses an *OPE* **(Objects-Properties-Events)** flowcharting system, which will be described in later projects.

5. **Write pseudocode for each event-triggered action.** *Pseudocode* is a specific but still English-like description of the steps that the program is to perform when a particular event occurs to a particular object. For example, you write pseudocode to describe what happens when the user clicks on a particular command button. Sometimes you must condense the pseudocode and combine it with the flowchart.

6. **Use the specification, pseudocode, and flowchart as guides while you develop actual Visual Basic source code for each event-triggered action.** The mechanics of using the Visual Basic language are described in upcoming projects.

7. **Run and test your program.** Correct any errors that may arise.

SYNTAX AND LOGIC ERRORS

Two general types of errors can occur when you are writing, testing, and using a program. During the early stages of development, you will occasionally make grammar mistakes, in the same way that an essay you submit for an English class may contain grammar errors ("She am driving to work"). You may mistype a variable name or keyword, use incorrect punctuation, and so forth. These grammar problems, called *syntax errors,* will be detected by the compiler and you will be prompted to fix them before Visual Basic will run your program to completion.

When you receive a syntax error message, pay close attention to the information that Visual Basic provides. Use the Help system to look up keywords that don't make sense to you. Errors sometimes have a cumulative effect on your program, where the first error may be causing others following it. In general, you should fix all errors, one at a time, and then run the program again. Once you have eliminated all syntax errors and your program is grammatically correct, you are ready for a full test of the program.

The real hassles of programming are not syntax errors but logic errors. A *logic error* (sometimes called a run-time error) is a mistake that causes your program to do something that you didn't intend. Logic errors correspond to submitting an essay for your English class that contains statements or ideas that you didn't really mean or intend: Your essay may be grammatically perfect but may not communicate what you wanted.

Often, programs will run without any syntax errors, but the program will still contain errors in output, calculation, or other areas. These logic errors are the infamous "bugs" in programs that can, depending on the program, lead to loss of money and time. Unfortunately, programming languages are not yet sophisticated enough to warn you about most logic errors because they do not understand what it is that your program is trying to do—that is, computers don't have common sense.

You can detect logic errors by carefully testing your program and checking its behavior in a variety of situations. Most large programs cannot be exhaustively tested, so there is always an element of risk. It has been said that no large program is ever perfect or bug-free. Your responsibility as a programmer is to make your programs as bug-free as possible. You should always perform reasonable, responsible testing of your programs to help ensure that logic errors are eliminated.

STARTING VISUAL BASIC

The standard name for the group window containing the Visual Basic program icon is Visual Basic 3.0, but your system could have a different name, like VB or VB 3.

 To start Visual Basic and resize the windows:

1 Open the group window containing the Visual Basic icon. Figure 0.3 shows an example of what you will see.

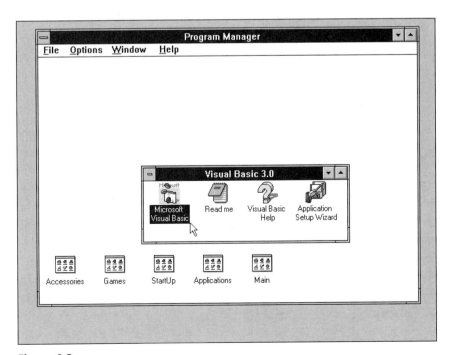

Figure 0.3

2 Double-click the Visual Basic icon.

> **Tip** Because Visual Basic uses several floating windows, it is a good idea to minimize the Program Manager window while you are using Visual Basic. This will prevent the screen from getting too cluttered.

3 Resize and move the windows so that the screen resembles Figure 0.4.

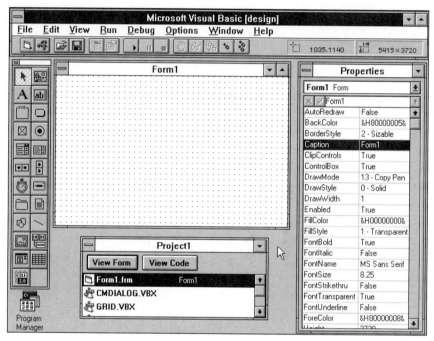

Figure 0.4

A QUICK LOOK AT THE VISUAL BASIC INTERFACE

Visual Basic uses an *IDE,* or *Integrated Development Environment.* The concept behind this IDE is that every tool needed to complete a Visual Basic program is available from this one environment. Only ten years ago, programmers would write and modify source code with a text editor program and then have to close the editor and compile the program with a separate compiler. If any errors occurred, the programmer would need to rerun the editor. Then, when there were no errors, the programmer would return to DOS and run the program. This could get monotonous and extremely time-consuming if there were many errors.

Modern programming languages, like Visual Basic, have dispensed with this problem by integrating the various stages of program development into one environment where all the tools you need are at hand.

There should be five windows on the screen once you have Visual Basic running: the Main window, the Form window, the Toolbox, the Project window, and the Properties window.

> ***Tip*** Sometimes when you begin a Visual Basic session, certain windows you need will not be on-screen. The toolbox, properties window, and project window can be activated by choosing them from the Tools menu.

You can arrange each of the windows to suit your working style and to best take advantage of the space available on-screen. For now, take a quick look at each window in Figure 0.5.

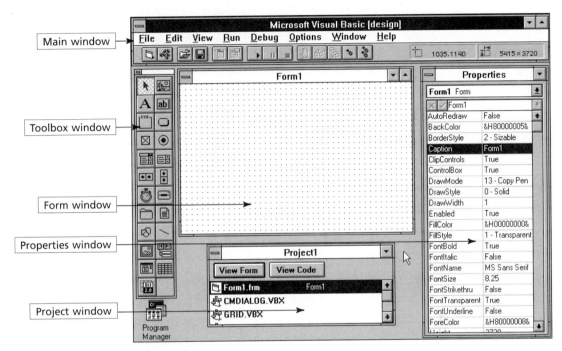

Figure 0.5

Main Window

The Main window contains the ***menu bar*** and ***toolbar***. The toolbar provides icons that allow quick access to commonly used commands. The buttons on the toolbar respond to a single mouse-click, similar to toolbar buttons in programs like Microsoft Word and Excel.

Toolbox

The Toolbox is a floating palette with buttons representing Visual Basic controls. Controls are selected by single-clicking the appropriate button. That control is then considered active and can be placed on the form window. Figure 0.6 details the names of each control on the Toolbox.

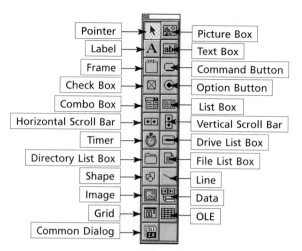

Figure 0.6

Form Window

The form is the basis, or backdrop, of your program. Each project can have one or more forms. Think of it as a blank slate: It's not much at first, but with a little creativity and the careful placing of objects, it can become anything. The placing of objects on a Form window is known as *painting,* similar to using a paintbrush to place colors on a canvas. The painting of controls on the form's surface is a primary aspect of Visual Basic interface design.

> **Reminder** A form is a window. What a Windows user would normally refer to as a *window* is called a *form* in Visual Basic. Don't be confused by the name: a form and a window are the same thing.

Properties Window

The Properties window is where each control on your form gets its attributes. The settings available in the Properties window vary depending on which control or form is selected. For example, a Label control, which is used to display text, has properties that specify the font, the text size, background and foreground color, and justification. The Properties window will quickly become familiar to you, and changing control properties will become second nature.

Project Window

The Project window lists the various files that make up the current *project,* as shown in Figure 0.5. While earlier versions of BASIC would typically use just one source code file per program, Visual Basic programs usually consist of several files. Visual Basic keeps track of all these files with a text file called a *project file* (sometimes called a **make file**). For this reason a complete Visual Basic program is called a **project.** A project can consist of numerous files that would be hard to organize manually. If you were to look at a project file, which has a .MAK extension, from a text editor like Windows Notepad, it might look something like Figure 0.7.

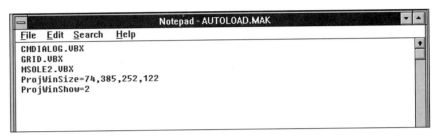

Figure 0.7

The Project window lists these files for you from within Visual Basic. If you look at the file list, you can see that your project has files that are included for you by Visual Basic. Most of the files are *VBXs,* or *Visual Basic custom controls.* These files define the controls that can be included in your program. The controls include the tools that appear in the Toolbox. There is even a default form named Form1 that is provided so you can get to work right away.

ACCESSING VISUAL BASIC HELP

The Help system in Visual Basic conforms to the standard Help conventions of Windows, which may be familiar to you if you have used other Windows applications. The Help system is like a vast reference manual stored on the hard disk, with indexing and cross-referencing capabilities. Help is a *hypertext* system, in which highlighted words can be selected to obtain more information. You can type a word naming the topic you're interested in, and Help will search its list of topics for that word. In the following steps you will use the Help menu to get information about Visual Basic forms.

To access the Help system:

1 Open the *Help* menu and choose *Search for Help On.*

2 Type **form** in the text box to get help with forms.
A list of form-related topics appears as shown in Figure 0.8.

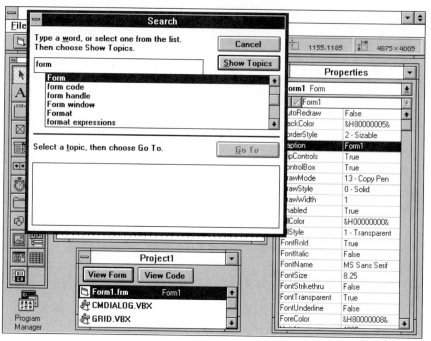

Figure 0.8

3 Click *Form window.*

4 Select **Show Topics.**

This action instructs Help to show the specific topics concerning Form windows for which it can provide help. As shown in Figure 0.9, several topics are displayed. The first topic, *Changing Grid Spacing*, is selected.

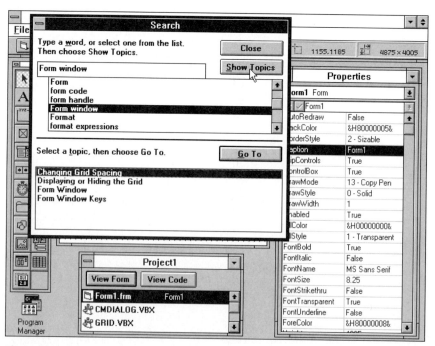

Figure 0.9

5 Select the topic *Form Window*.

6 Select **Go To**.

Help information about the Form window appears.

7 Click the word *application*. A small window defining the term is revealed, as shown in Figure 0.10.

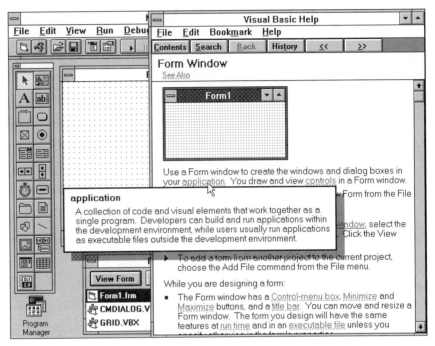

Figure 0.10

8 Select the **Contents** button near the top of the Help window. Help's Table of Contents appears. To read about one of the available topics, simply select that topic.

9 Open the **File** menu and choose **Exit**.

You have exited Visual Basic Help.

EXITING VISUAL BASIC

You will now exit Visual Basic.

To exit Visual Basic:

1 Open the **File** menu and choose **Exit**.

The Save Form dialog box appears.

2 Because you have not yet created a form you want to save, select **No**.

3 Select **No** in the Save Project1 dialog box if it appears.

If you prefer, you can exit Visual Basic by double-clicking the Control-menu box in the upper-left corner of the Main window. The smaller Control-menu box closes only the current project, not the Visual Basic program.

Tip One of the things that is saved when you choose Save Project is the location and size of all the Visual Basic windows, so that your customized environment returns to the way you want it when you reopen the project later. If you happen to close the Form window and then save the project, the next time you open that project, the Form window will not appear. This can be confusing. If you open a project that you have previously saved, and the form does not appear, select the form from the project window to open it.

THE NEXT STEP

You are about to enter the exciting world of Windows program creation using Visual Basic. In Project 1 you will build a program that uses no programmer-written code at all. Your first program will display formatted text in a window—not earth-shattering by any means, but a true achievement for any beginning programmer nonetheless.

This concludes the Overview. You can either exit Visual Basic or go on to work the Study Questions.

SUMMARY AND EXERCISES

Summary

- A program is a series of instructions for a computer, written with a programming language.
- Visual Basic allows easy and powerful event-driven programming for the Windows operating system.
- Syntax errors are the grammar errors of programming.
- Logic errors, or run-time errors, occur when the program does not run according to specification.
- A typical Visual Basic programming environment will have five windows: Main, Toolbox, Form, Properties, and Project.
- The Main window contains the menu bar and toolbar.
- The Toolbox is a floating palette of controls.
- The Form window is where controls are painted and manipulated. It represents what the program will look like to the user.
- The Properties window is used to change attributes for the various controls and forms that your project uses.
- The Project window lists the files that make up the current project.
- The Visual Basic Help system provides an extensive online reference manual.

Key Terms and Operations

Key Terms

code compatibility
compiler
control
event-driven programming
execute
form
hypertext
IDE (Integrated Development
    Environment)
interpreter
logic error
machine code
machine language
make file
menu bar
object
OPE (Objects-Properties-Events)
p-code
packed code

painting
program
programmer
programming language
project
project file
properties
pseudocode
run
source code
syntax error
toolbar
VBX (Visual Basic custom control)

Operations

Access online Help
Exit Visual Basic
Minimize the Program Manager
    window
Organize windows
Start Visual Basic

Study Questions

Multiple Choice

1. In Visual Basic terminology, a window is called a
    a. file.
    b. form.
    c. window.
    d. project.
    e. pseudocode.

2. Visual Basic is a curious hybrid of which two types of language translators?
    a. machine and octal
    b. compiled and debugged
    c. notated and annotated
    d. interpreted and compiled
    e. linker and source browser

3. The human-readable program, as written in a particular programming language by the programmer, is called
    a. source code.
    b. machine code.
    c. machine language.
    d. p-code.
    e. a data segment.

4. The programming concept Visual Basic uses is called
    a. procedural.
    b. timer-driven.
    c. event-driven.
    d. Gatesian.
    e. modal.

5. Which window is a palette of controls?
   a. Properties window
   b. Toolbox window
   c. Main window
   d. Project window
   e. Form window

Short Answer

1. What is the native language of the computer?

2. What is the user clicking a command button an example of?

3. A grammar error, such as the misspelling of a keyword, is an example of what type of error?

4. A program that does not conform to the user's specifications, or does not otherwise run as expected, is called what type of error?

For Discussion

1. How is Visual Basic different than traditional BASIC languages?

2. What are the drawbacks to Visual Basic's ease of use?

3. How does the event-driven style of programming affect the programmer?

4. Why is event-driven programming a natural for Windows software development?

PROJECT 1: BUILDING YOUR FIRST PROGRAM

Objectives

After completing this project, you should be able to:

▶ Create and save a Visual Basic project

▶ Place text on a form

▶ Change form and text control properties

▶ Run Visual Basic programs from the IDE

▶ Print and read a program listing

▶ Create an EXE file and run that program from Windows

CASE STUDY: HELLO, WORLD!

The primary purpose of this first program is to acquaint you with the Visual Basic programming environment by providing some hands-on experience. One of the most exciting aspects of Visual Basic programming is its ability to generate working programs for which the programmer has to write little or no actual source code.

Using only controls and properties, you will create your first real Windows application. The program you create will be fairly modest: It will display the phrase *Hello, world!* in the middle of a small window.

Designing the Solution

The specifications for this first program are as follows:

- The program will display a window whose title bar contains your name followed by a colon, a space, and the phrase *Project 1*.
- The window will have a fixed double border so that it cannot be resized.
- The background color of the window will be bright yellow.
- In the approximate center of the window, the phrase *Hello, world!* will be displayed in the Times New Roman font, 24-point bold italic.
- The foreground color (that is, the color of the letters) of the *Hello, world!* text will be deep blue, and the background will be bright yellow to match the form background.

A hand-drawn sketch of the interface might look like Figure 1.1.

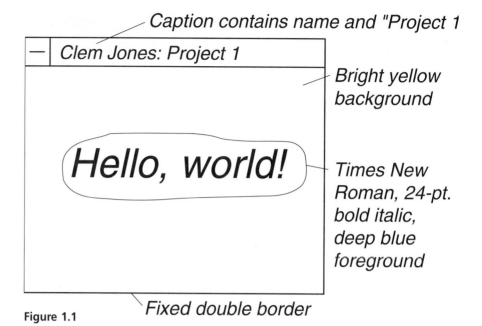

Figure 1.1

Because this first program does not involve writing code to respond to specific events, there is no need to describe events or write pseudocode for them.

STARTING AND SAVING A NEW PROJECT

Visual Basic works with two primary file types: project files, also called **MAK files,** and form files, also called **FRM files.** Projects are saved from the Save Project option in the File menu. Forms are saved from the Save File option.

Forms are saved separately from projects because they are reusable. Consider the Save dialog box that all Windows programs use. This is a reusable form supplied by Microsoft that all programmers, yourself included, can use. If this wasn't the case, everyone who needed the save capability for their programs would need to write their own Save dialog box.

> **Reminder** A form is an essential part of a Visual Basic project, but it is saved separate from the project so that it can be reused by other projects if necessary. Form files are stored separately on the disk.

It is important to name and save both types of files as an early step in developing a Visual Basic project.

To start and save a Visual Basic project:

1 Open the group window containing the Visual Basic icon.

2 Double-click the Visual Basic icon to start Visual Basic.

3 Resize and move the windows as you did in the Overview, so the screen resembles Figure 1.2.

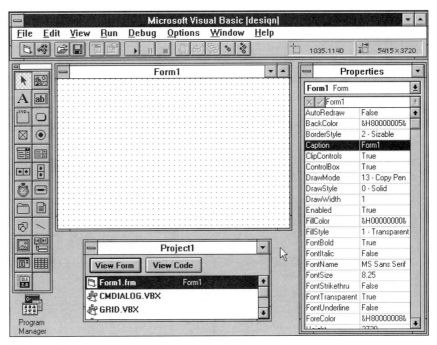

Figure 1.2

4 Choose **File,** and then choose **Save Project.**
A Save File As dialog box appears. You will save the form file here, as
shown in Figure 1.3.

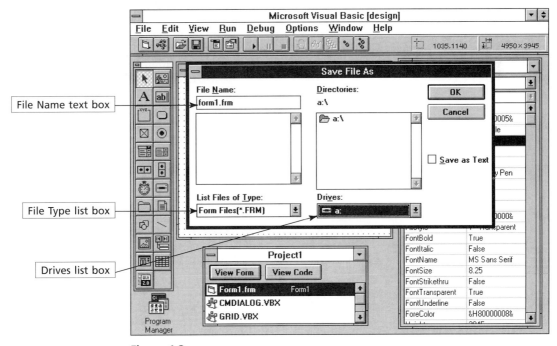

Figure 1.3

5 Use the **Drives** list box to change to drive A.

Reminder If you are not using drive A, remember to substitute the drive and path you are using instead.

6 Double-click the **File Name** text box; then type HELLO and select **OK.** The form file is saved on drive A under the name HELLO.FRM. A dialog box for saving the project file then appears.

7 Type HELLO in the **File Name** text box and select **OK,** as shown in Figure 1.4.

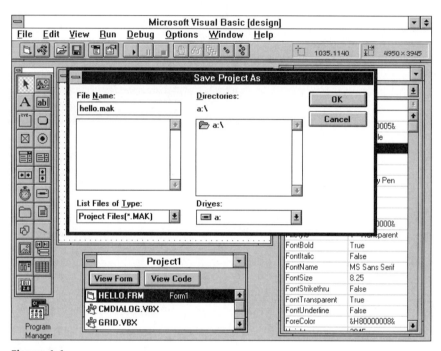

Figure 1.4

The project file is saved under the name HELLO.MAK. You will notice that the title bar of the Project window changes to reflect the new filename, as has the filename for Form1 within the Project window.

Tip Changing the form filename does not change the title on the Form window. It only changes the filename as seen by the file system. Changing the title on the Form window requires changing a form property, which is covered later in the project.

CHANGING PROPERTIES

The Properties window contains an alphabetical list of attributes for the selected object. There are various ways to change individual properties. Clicking the property name once will select it and place the current value for that property in the Settings box near the top of the Properties window. In Figure 1.5 the Caption property is selected, and Form1, its current value, is shown in the Settings box.

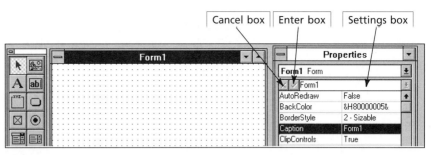

Figure 1.5

By clicking the Settings box once, you can edit the text and, in this case, change the caption for Form1. The buttons to the left of the Settings box that resemble an *X* and a check mark are called the Cancel and Enter boxes, respectively you can use these buttons to confirm any changes you make in the Settings box. If you want to accept the changes, you can press (ENTER) or click the Enter box. If you decide not to keep any change you may have made, clicking the Cancel box will return that property's setting to its previous value.

You can also double-click a property name in the Properties window to cycle that property through each of its possible settings. For example, the ControlBox property, as shown in Figure 1.6 has only two settings: True and False. If you double-click the ControlBox property, it will change to False. If you double-click again, it will change back to True.

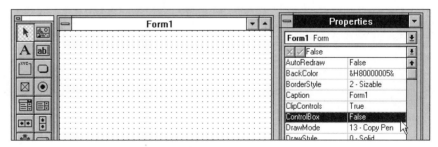

Figure 1.6

For properties that have multiple settings, the double-click method may prove tiring if the selection you want does not appear quickly. For example, the FontName property will typically have many possible settings. To select one of the fonts quickly, you can click the FontName setting once to select it. A drop-down list box will appear to the right of the Settings box. You can then click this list box to display a list of available fonts, as shown in Figure 1.7.

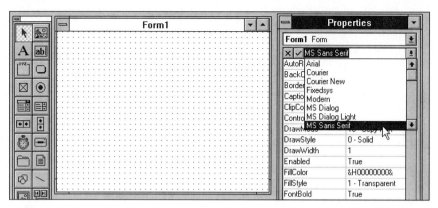

Figure 1.7

The method you choose to change property settings will depend on your personal preference and the property you are changing. In this project you will be guided through the steps needed to change properties. In later projects, as you become more comfortable with the Visual Basic interface, you will be instructed simply to change a property setting, and you can choose the technique you prefer.

Changing the Caption Property

You will now change the Caption property for the form. The caption property is used to set the text that displays in the form's title bar. Notice that the caption is now Form1.

> **Tip** Before changing any properties, you should always make sure that you select the object whose properties you want to affect. You select an object by clicking it once with the mouse.

To change the Caption property:

1 Click anywhere in Form1 to select the form.

2 In the Properties window, double-click the **Caption** property. The text in the Settings box is highlighted, meaning that you may change it.

3 Type your name, a colon, a space, and `Project 1`
The screen should resemble Figure 1.8, with your name replacing *Clem Jones*.

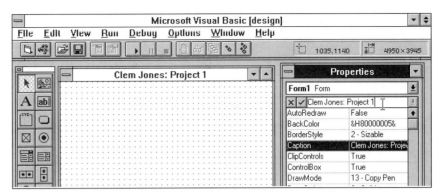

Figure 1.8

 4 Click the Enter box or press (ENTER)
The new caption appears on the Form window title bar as you type.

RUNNING THE PROGRAM

Though you have made only one small change to the default form, you can still try running your program.

 ### To run the program from the IDE:

 1 Run the program by clicking the Run button on the toolbar or by choosing **Start** from the **Run** menu.
As shown in Figure 1.9, the program is now running.

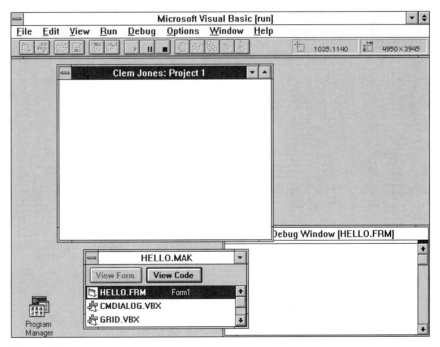

Figure 1.9

2 Experiment with resizing and moving your the Project's window, as shown in Figure 1.10.

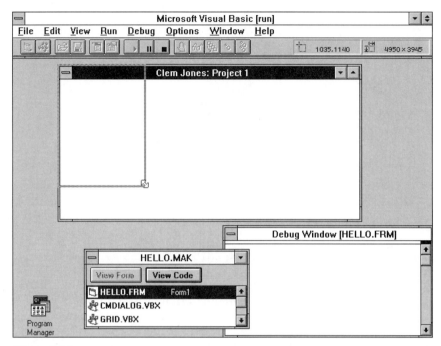

Figure 1.10

3 Double-click *your program's* control-menu box (not the Control-menu box in the Visual Basic Main window) to stop the program.

CHANGING THE BORDERSTYLE PROPERTY

You will recall from the specifications for this program given earlier in the project, the window will not be resizable. This is a property of the form that you can easily change.

You may want to experiment with various border styles and see how they affect the look of your program. Making changes to your program and rerunning it to see how those changes affect the appearance of your interface is quick and easy with Visual Basic.

To change the BorderStyle property:

1 Click within the Form window to select it.

2 Click the **BorderStyle** property in the Properties window.
Notice that the current border style displayed in the Settings box is 2 - Sizable. You can open a pull-down list box to select a different border style.

3 Open the BorderStyle list box and choose the **3 - Fixed Double** style, as shown in Figure 1.11.

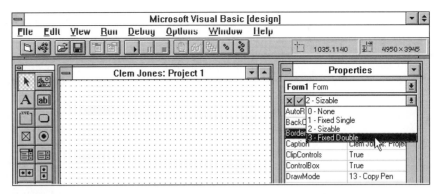

Figure 1.11

The Fixed Double border style does not immediately appear on the form, because you are still allowed to resize the form while you are designing it. When the program runs, however, the Form window will have a fixed double-line border.

4 Click the run button on the toolbar to run the program.
Notice that the window can still be moved, but it cannot be resized.

5 Double-click the Control-menu box to stop the program.

CHANGING THE BACKGROUND COLOR PROPERTY

Next, you will change the background color (BackColor) property of the form to add a little visual flair to your program.

To change the BackColor property:

1 Click within the Form window to select it.
Do not click on one of the existing controls. You must click on a blank unused area.

2 Double-click the **BackColor** property in the Properties window.

3 Select yellow by clicking on that color, as shown in Figure 1.12.

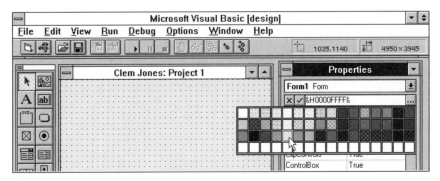

Figure 1.12

EXIT If necessary, you can save your work, exit Visual Basic, and continue this project later.

VISUAL BASIC OBJECT-NAMING CONVENTIONS

Charles Simonyi, a famous programmer from Xerox PARC, and later, Microsoft, invented the so-called *Hungarian naming convention* that is prevalent in programming today. In Hungarian notation object names are given a descriptive prefix so that the meaning of the object is obvious. A form name in Visual Basic, for example, is preceded by the prefix *frm*. If you were writing a program that used a form for displaying a message, you might call it frmDisplayMsg. The name is descriptive, and the prefix *frm* tells you that the object is a form.

This naming style will become more important when you write actual Visual Basic code in later projects. Some common naming prefixes in Visual Basic are as follows:

Object	Prefix
Form	frm
Command button	cmd
Label	lbl
Menu	mnu

You will be introduced to more object name prefixes as you continue to work through the projects and new objects are introduced.

Charles Simonyi, by the way, *is* from Hungary, and the name Hungarian notation is something of an inside joke to him. Code written in Hungarian notation looks like gibberish to those who have not been introduced to the style. It is only when you understand how it works that Hungarian notation becomes easy to read.

Changing the Name Property

The name Form1 is not very descriptive. You will give your form a descriptive name, using the naming conventions described in the previous section.

To change the Name property:

1 Click within the Form window to select it.

2 Scroll down the Properties list until the **Name** property appears.

3 Double-click the **Name** property in the Properties window.

4 Type the new name frmHello and press (ENTER)

The screen should look like Figure 1.13. Notice that the form name also changes in the Project window.

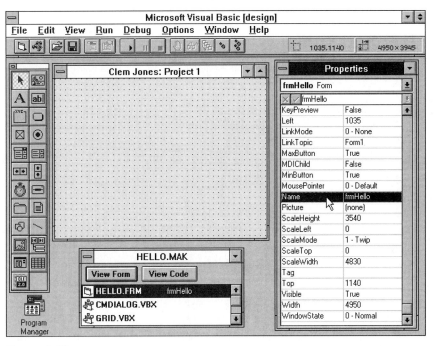

Figure 1.13

CREATING A LABEL CONTROL

Remember, there are no events for this program, so the next object to create is a **Label control** that will be used to display the *Hello, world!* message. A Label control is used to display text that cannot be directly edited by the user. This text is called a **caption.**

> **Tip** Many Visual Basic objects have a Caption property; Label controls and forms are just two examples. Both of those objects display text that is for output only. You will find that many objects share common properties and that these properties work in similar ways regardless of the object that is selected.

Label controls can be added with the Label button (the one that looks like a capital *A*) in the Toolbox.

To create a Label control:

1 Click the Label tool, as shown in Figure 1.14.

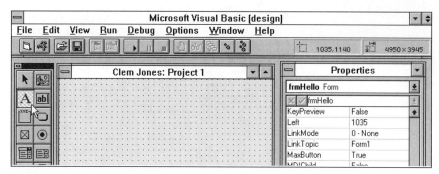

Figure 1.14

The tool is highlighted, indicating that it is currently active. You can use it to trace out an area on the form where you want a label to appear.

2 Move the mouse pointer inside the form.
The pointer appears as crosshairs.

3 Position the crosshairs about an inch from the upper-left corner of the form, hold down the mouse button, and drag it across the form, as shown in Figure 1.15.

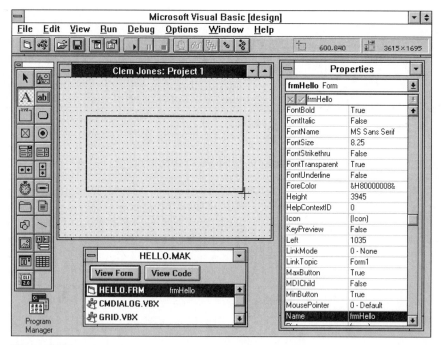

Figure 1.15

4 Release the mouse button.
A Label control now exists on top of the form. The screen should resemble Figure 1.16.

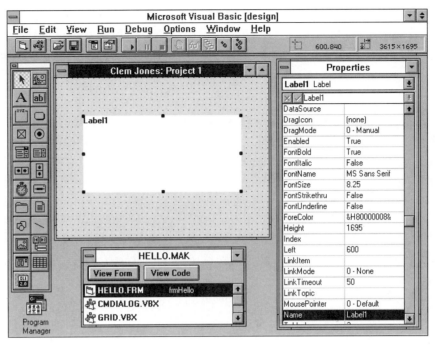

Figure 1.16

Tip When selecting controls from the Toolbox, you can also double-click the control you want. This action places that control in the center of the current form, with a default size. The control can then be moved and resized as desired.

Changing Label Control Properties

The label has the default caption Label1, but you will be change this to the phrase *Hello, world!* You can tell that the Label control is selected because it is surrounded by small black boxes, called **handles,** that can be used to resize the control. The control can also be moved by clicking and dragging it, similar to moving a window.

In the steps that follow you will change the properties of the Label control.

To change the Label control properties:

1 Click the Form window but in a blank area away from the label. The form is selected, and its Properties list appears. This is not what you want.

2 Click the Label control.
Now the Label control is selected, and *its* Properties list appears.

Caution It is very important to make sure you have selected the correct object before changing properties.

3 Double-click the **BackColor** property of the Label control, and select the same yellow used in the background of frmHello.

4 Double-click the foreground color property, **ForeColor,** and select blue.

This will be the color in which the label caption is displayed. Notice that the phrase *Label1* changes color.

5 Double-click the **Caption** property; then type `Hello, world!` and press (ENTER). The screen should look like Figure 1.17.

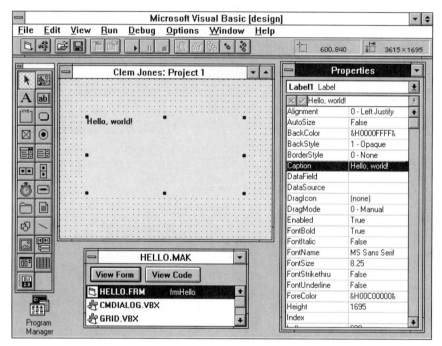

Figure 1.17

6 Make sure that the Label control is still selected, click the **FontName** property, open the drop-down list box to see a list of fonts, scroll down the list, and select **Times New Roman.**

7 Click the **FontSize** property, and use the list box to select a size of 24 points.

Notice that the FontBold property is already set to True.

8 Click the **FontItalic** property, and use the list box to select **True.**

9 Click the **Alignment** property, and use the list box to select **Center.** The screen should now resemble Figure 1.18.

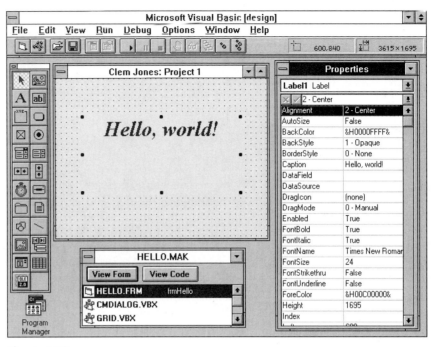

Figure 1.18

10 Double-click the **Name** property of the label, and then type **lbl-Hello.**
The prefix *lbl* is used to designate that this object is a label.

SAVING AND RUNNING THE PROGRAM

It is important to save your project after you have made significant changes. Remember that you cannot save too often. Once you have saved your project, then you can see what you have created.

 To save and run the program:

 1 Click the **Save** button on the toolbar, as shown in Figure 1.19. This action saves both the project file and the form file.

Figure 1.19

2 Click the Run button on the toolbar to run the program. Check that it works as the specifications require.

3 Make corrections and rerun if necessary.

4 Double-click the Project window Control-menu box to stop the program.

CREATING AN EXE FILE

If you would like to execute your program outside of the Visual Basic environment, you must create an *EXE,* or executable, file first. This will, for the most part, allow your program to run from the File Manager or from an icon in the Program Manager, just like any other Windows program.

Actually, Visual Basic does not create stand-alone programs. Executable files created with Visual Basic 3.0 also require that the file VBRUN300.DLL be present on the system on which you will be running your program. VBRUN300.DLL comes free with Visual Basic and is placed automatically in the directory C:\WINDOWS\SYSTEM when Visual Basic is installed.

> *Tip* Earlier versions of Visual Basic for Windows require files similar to VBRUN300.DLL. Programs written with Visual Basic version 1.0 require the file VBRUN100.DLL. Programs written with version 2.0 require VBRUN200.DLL.

To run your program on a Windows-based computer that does not have Visual Basic, you must copy VBRUN300.DLL to that computer as well. Because of the popularity of Visual Basic, many computers will already have the file VBRUN300.DLL installed.

To create a Visual Basic EXE file:

1 Choose **File** and then choose **Make EXE File.**
The Make EXE File dialog box appears, as shown in Figure 1.20.

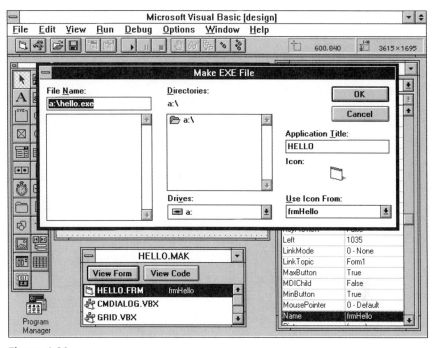

Figure 1.20

2 If the drive is not set to A, use the **Drives** list box to change to drive A.

3 Double-click the **File Name** text box; then type **HELLO** and select **OK.** This creates an executable file, HELLO.EXE, on the diskette in drive A. You may run this program the same way that you would run any other Windows program.

Running a Visual Basic EXE File from Outside the IDE

Now that you have created an EXE file, your program can be executed from outside the Visual Basic environment. To check this, you will run your program from the File Manager.

To run your program from the File Manager:

1 Minimize the Visual Basic IDE.

2 Maximize the Program Manager window by double-clicking the Program Manager icon in the lower-left corner of the screen.

3 Open the Main program group and start the File Manager program by double-clicking the File Manager icon.

4 Select drive A.

5 Double-click the program HELLO.EXE to execute your program. It's alive! The screen should look similar to Figure 1.21.

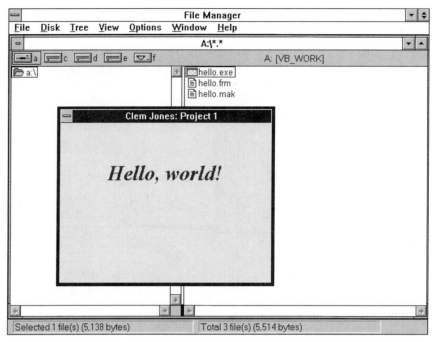

Figure 1.21

6 Close File Manager and exit your program as usual. You should also minimize Program Manager and return to the Visual Basic IDE.

PRINTING A PROGRAM LISTING

Visual Basic can print a picture of the forms in the current project, the form text, the program code, or any combination of the three. Before you print, you should check your printer to make sure that it is turned on, has paper, and is online (communicating with the computer).

To print a program listing, you will use the Print option on the File menu. The Print dialog box appears, as shown in Figure 1.22, with three check boxes: Form, Form Text, and Code. The Form option will cause Visual Basic to print an image of the form on a page by itself. The Form Text option will print a list of the properties for the form and each of the controls that are on the form. Selecting Code will print a source code listing of all the event procedures in your program.

The Print dialog box also includes two buttons: Current and All. You will click Current to print just the currently selected form. Some Visual Basic projects will have more than one form, however. Selecting the All option button will cause Visual Basic to print information from every form in your project.

To print a program listing and exit Visual Basic:

1 Make sure the printer is ready.

2 Choose **File** and then **Print.**
The Print dialog box appears as shown in Figure 1.22.

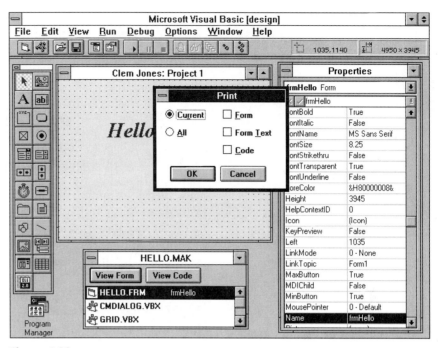

Figure 1.22

As you can see, there are three check boxes that you can use to select which portions of the project you would like to print.

3 Select **Form** and **Form Text.** Since this project has no code to print, checking Code is unnecessary.

4 Select **OK.**

5 Choose **File** and then **Exit.**
A dialog box appears asking if you would like to save changes to the project file.

6 If you are sure that you have not made any changes to Project 1 since the last time you saved, you may choose **No.** Otherwise, choose **Yes.** Visual Basic saves your project and closes.

THE NEXT STEP

Now that you have gotten acquainted with the Visual Basic environment and have created your first Visual Basic program, you are ready to create more advanced applications. In Project 2 you will create HELLO2, a program that will add interactive user input, command buttons, and other enhancements to the original HELLO project. You will also write some actual Visual Basic code for the first time.

This concludes Project 1. You can either exit Visual Basic or go on to work the Study Questions, Review Exercises, and Assignments.

SUMMARY AND EXERCISES

Summary

- Projects and forms are saved separately.
- The Caption property is used to change the text in a Label control.
- The BorderStyle property specifies a form's border.
- BackColor sets the background color for forms and controls.
- The Name property sets the internal name for a form or control. There are specific naming conventions designed to make Visual Basic program listings easier to read.
- The Label control allows your program to output text.
- Visual Basic programs can be run from inside the IDE, or they can be made into EXE files that can run directly under Windows.
- You can print forms, form text, and code.

Key Terms and Operations

Key Terms	Operations
caption	Create an EXE file
EXE file	Create controls with the Toolbox
form	Print a program listing
FRM file	Run a program from within the IDE
handles	
Hungarian naming convention	Run an EXE file from Windows
Label control	Save a project separately from a form
MAK file	
	Use the Properties window to change object properties

Study Questions

Multiple Choice

1. The form is saved separately from the project because
   a. it is compiled.
   b. it can be reused.
   c. it is document-centric.
   d. it can be indented.
   e. of the code segment.

2. The Label control is used to
   a. call a subprogram.
   b. allow input.
   e. name a variable.
   d. name the title bar.
   e. display text.

3. What are the two primary file types that Visual Basic works with?
   a. EXE and COM
   b. FRM and MAK
   c. FOR and MAK
   d. FOR and NXT
   e. ASM and PAS

4. Which window contains an alphabetical list of attributes for the currently selected object?
   a. Form window
   b. Project window
   c. Visual Basic window
   d. Main window
   e. Properties window

5. Double-clicking a property in the properties list will
   a. dial the modem.
   b. move to the next property in the list.
   c. cycle through the available choices for that property.
   d. change the focus to the Project window.
   e. have no effect.

6. To test your program (have Visual Basic run your code) from within the IDE, you can choose
   a. File and Run.
   b. File and Make Exe File.
   c. Run and Start.
   d. Run and Break.
   e. Test and Begin.

7. If you don't want the user to resize your program's window, which property would you change?
   a. Caption
   b. BorderStyle
   c. BorderType
   d. Resize
   e. ResizeStyle

8. Using Hungarian notation, the prefix for a form name?
   a. form
   b. from
   c. f
   d. for
   e. frm

9. The property used to identify an object is called the
   a. Title property.
   b. Name property.
   c. Caption property.
   d. Label property.
   e. InternalName property.

10. The text in a Label control is to consist of green letters on a red background. Which two properties would need to be modified to produce the color change?
   a. FontColor and BackColor
   b. TextColor and BackColor
   c. FontColor and BGColor
   d. ForeColor and BackColor
   e. ForeColor and FormColor

Short Answer

1. How do you create an EXE file?

2. How would you change a form's border style to fixed width, unsizable?

3. Why should controls and forms in Visual Basic have unique names?

4. Which property specifies the text that will appear in the title bar of a form?

5. In the Hungarian naming convention, the prefix that the programmer attaches to an object name serves to remind him or her of what?

6. Which property describes the text that appears in a Label control or a form's title bar?

7. Will the Alignment property affect the alignment of text relative to the edges of the selected object or relative to the form?

8. If you would like to distribute a Visual Basic program you created to another Windows user, which additional file must you include with your executable file?

9. What three-letter file extension represents an executable version of your program?

10. What is a printout of your program's listing called?

For Discussion

1. The program you created in this project did not require you to write any code. Describe the general process that you did follow to create the program.

2. Even though Visual Basic doesn't require you to use the Hungarian naming convention, it is still a common practice for the programmer. Why?

3. Is an executable file created by the Visual Basic compiler a completely stand-alone program? Explain.

Review Exercises

Creating an Address Form

Design a form that displays your name and address in Arial 18-point bold type with a red background and yellow foreground. Allow the form to be resizable. Experiment with resizing the form to see what effect resizing has on the displayed text.

Practicing With Properties

Try to duplicate the font and alignment of the form and controls shown in Figure 1.23. The background of the form should be blue, and the Label backgrounds should be green. The foreground color for the labels should be white.

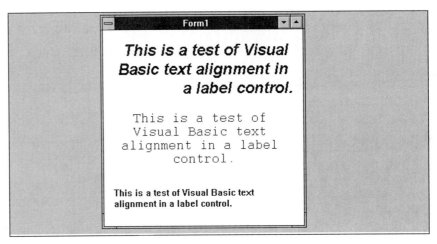

Figure 1.23

Assignments

Writing Specifications

Sometimes specifications resemble clear instructions that might be given to a person so that he or she could perform a certain task. Write specifications that will compute gross pay based on the following information:

1. The pay rate is $5.00 per hour.

2. Hours above 40 are paid at a rate of one and a half times the pay rate.

PROJECT 2: MODIFYING AND ENHANCING A PROGRAM

Objectives

After completing this project, you should be able to:

▶ Modify an existing project

▶ Position and resize controls on a form

▶ Create command buttons

▶ Attach code to event procedures

▶ Create text boxes

▶ Use the If-Then-Else statement

CASE STUDY: IMPROVING THE HELLO PROGRAM

While Visual Basic's ability to create a running program without any code is a powerful feature, it has limitations. The HELLO program you created in Project 1 offers no interaction with the user. The only method of quitting the program is through the Control-menu box. Most Windows programs are more powerful than that. To produce a more useful program, you will need to write some Visual Basic code. As you will see, Visual Basic code is logical and easy to understand.

In this project you will produce an enhanced version of your first program. This version of the HELLO program will allow the user to input his or her name. It will then use the name to display a greeting to the user. You will also add command buttons to increase the usability of the program.

Designing the Solution

You will modify the program from Project 1 so that it allows the user to enter a name, and, upon clicking a button labeled Greeting, see the name combined with the greeting *Hello* and an exclamation point. For example, if the user types *Clem* for the name and clicks the Greeting button, the words *Hello, Clem!* will be displayed.

In the new program you will also include a Clear button that blanks out any displayed greeting and any entered text. A Close button will also be included to allow the user to exit the program without using the Control-menu box.

This program should respond to the following events:

- Clicking the Greeting button
- Clicking the Clear button
- Clicking the Close button

You can use these specifications to sketch the Form window and its controls.

Using the OPE Flowchart

In this project you will enhance the HELLO program to include other events needed for the program to run smoothly. The OPE flowchart in Figure 2.1 mentions some of these events; you can refer to the flowchart as you complete the steps of the project. As you can see, the OPE flowchart is particularly suited to the event-driven Visual Basic environment. OPE, an acronym for Objects-Properties-Events, embodies the very concept behind Visual Basic in a clear and concise way.

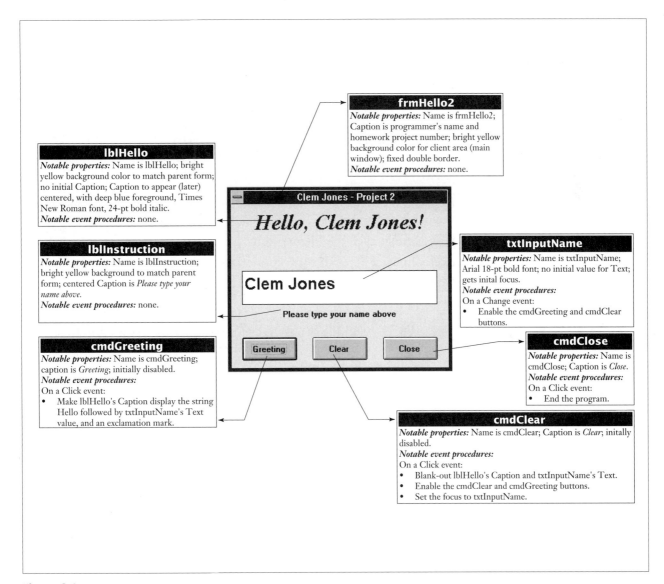

Figure 2.1

CREATING A NEW PROGRAM FROM A COMPLETED ONE

Since the new program will be an enhancement of the HELLO program you created in Project 1, you will be able to use some of the work you completed in the first project. The first steps will involve saving copies of the Project 1 project (MAK) and form (FRM) files under new names for Project 2 so that they will not be confused with Project 1.

To create and save a new file:

1 Start Visual Basic, and minimize the Program Manager.

2 Choose **File,** and then choose **Open Project.**

3 Change disk drives and directories if necessary, select HELLO.MAK, and then select **OK.**
If you already have a project open, you will be prompted to save it. Decide whether you want to, and then proceed to open HELLO.MAK.

View Form

4 If frmHello does not appear, click the **View Form** button in the Project window.

> *Tip* Often, when you reopen a previously saved project, you will not see the form window displayed. This can be confusing, and even a little scary, since it seems as if the form has been lost. Remember that you can use the View Form button on the Project window to display the form.

5 If the Properties window is not already visible, choose **Window,** and then choose **Properties.**

6 Double-click the **Name** property and type the new name `frmHello2`

7 Choose **File,** and then choose **Save Project As.**

8 Type the new project name `HELLO2.MAK` and then select **OK.**

> *Tip* When saving filenames, it is not necessary to add file extensions. The Save Project As dialog box will automatically add the .MAK extension to filenames if you do not do so. Likewise, the Save File As dialog box defaults to the .FRM extension.

9 Choose **File,** and then choose **Save File As.**

10 Type the new form name `HELLO2.FRM` and then select **OK.**

11 Make sure the form is selected, double-click the **Caption** property, and type **Project 2** in the Settings box, as shown in Figure 2.2.
Now you are ready to begin.

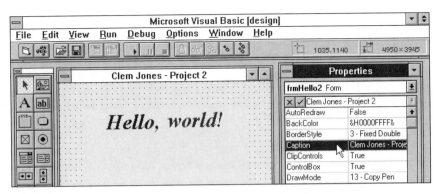

Figure 2.2

CHANGING THE lblHELLO LABEL CONTROL

The first change you will make is to move the lblHello Label control to the top of the form to make room for the other controls.

To move the Label control:

1 Select lblHello by clicking the control directly, and then drag it to the top of the form, as shown in Figure 2.3.

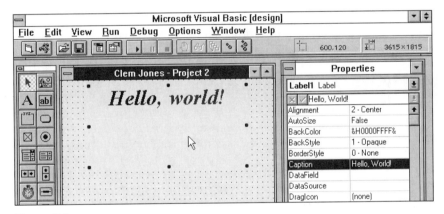

Figure 2.3

2 Resize lblHello so that it does not take up as much space, as shown in Figure 2.4.

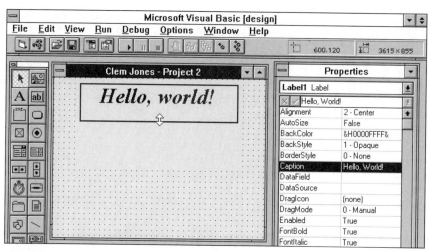

Figure 2.4

The caption for lblHello will appear only after the user clicks the Greeting command button. Initially, the caption will be blank.

To change the Caption property to blank:

1 Backspace over the caption text in the Properties window to delete the *Hello, world!* greeting.

2 Press (ENTER) to continue.
The caption is now blank.

ADDING A COMMAND BUTTON

Command buttons provide the user with an easy way to cause an action to occur. Typical command buttons have captions like OK and Cancel. When a command button, or push button as it is sometimes called, is selected, it appears to be pushed in.

A *click event procedure* which occurs whenever the user presses a mouse button, is processed, or *called,* when a command button is pressed by the user in this case. You will add code to the click event procedure that will occur in response to the user pressing the command button.

To add a command button:

1 Double-click the Command Button Tool in the Toolbox.
A command button will appear in the center of frmHello2, as shown in Figure 2.5.

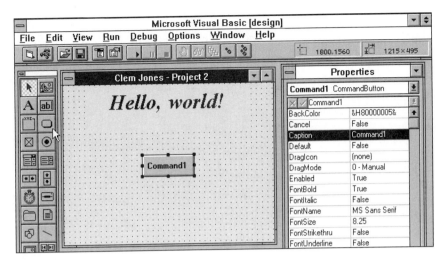

Figure 2.5

2 Drag the command button to the lower-left corner of frmHello2, as shown in Figure 2.6.

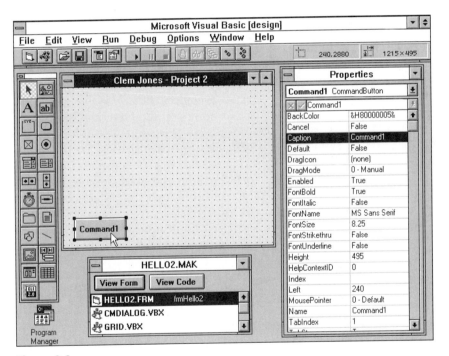

Figure 2.6

3 Make sure the command button is selected, double-click the **Caption** property, and then type **Greeting**
The prefix for command button names is *cmd*.

4 Double-click the **Name** property for the command button and type **cmdGreeting**
The screen should resemble Figure 2.7.

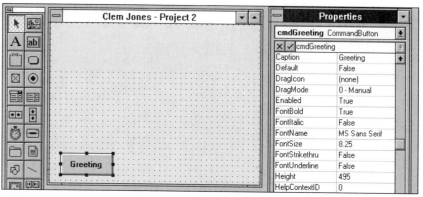

Figure 2.7

5 Run the program, and click the Greeting button.

Notice that nothing happens. This occurs because you have not yet written any code indicating what should happen when the button is clicked.

6 Stop the program.

WRITING AN EVENT PROCEDURE

Thus far, all the code for your program has been generated for you by Visual Basic. You will now write your own code: You will specify the *event procedure,* or *subroutine,* that should execute when a mouse-click event occurs on the Greeting button.

An event procedure is simply a block of program code that executes whenever a particular event occurs. Each event triggers a procedure. Clicking the mouse on a command button, for example, triggers a *click procedure* for the command button object. A click procedure is simply a type of event procedure that occurs when the user clicks on any control or form object.

If you think about it, Windows is nothing more than a series of events. The mouse is clicked, objects are selected; even mouse movement and location are events. Obviously, you cannot respond to *every* event. Your program should only respond to the events that affect it. Even then, the number of events can be enormous, and most of those events are superfluous. The goal is to filter the events and respond to the ones that are important to *your* program.

To create the event procedure:

1 Select the Greeting button in the Form window.

2 Double-click the Greeting button.

As shown in Figure 2.8, this action opens the *Code window.* The Code window is where you will type in actual program code.

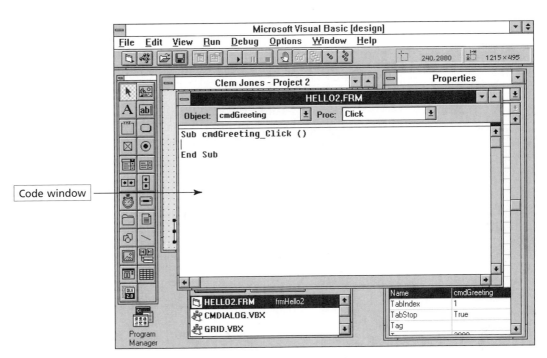

Code window

Figure 2.8

Notice that drop-down list boxes in the Code window allow you to
select from among various objects (for example, the controls on your
form) and, for a particular object, the **proc**, or event procedure, for which
you wish to write code. As shown in Figure 2.8, the current object is
cmdGreeting, the default current event procedure is *Click*, and the standard
name given to the subroutine code is *cmdGreeting_Click*. Every time a
click event occurs on the cmdGreeting button, this subroutine will execute.

The greeting *Hello, world!* should appear as the caption for lblHello
when the user clicks the cmdGreeting button. To do this, you need to set
the Caption property for lblHello to *Hello, world!* by writing Visual Basic
code. Visual Basic uses specific syntax when determining how properties
are set using code. An object's property can be referred to by using the
ObjectName.PropertyName convention. For example, lblHello.Caption
means "Hello Label's Caption property," where the dot is almost like the
possessive *'s* in English.

 ### To add code to the Code window:

1 Type `lblHello.Caption = "Hello, world!"` inside the subroutine,
as shown in Figure 2.9.

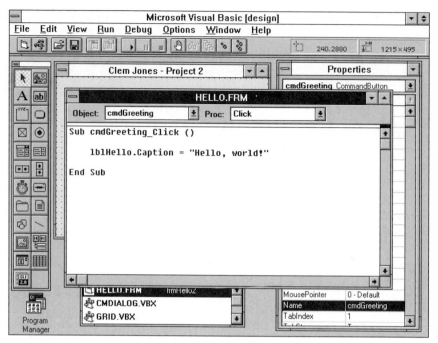

Figure 2.9

 Double-click the Code window's Control-menu box to close the Code window.

3 Run the program.

4 Click the Greeting button, and the greeting *Hello, world!* should appear near the top of the window.

5 Stop the program.
Congratulations! You've written your first Visual Basic code and have seen its effect on your program.

EXIT If necessary, you can save your work, exit Visual Basic, and continue this project later.

ENCOUNTERING A RUN-TIME ERROR

Sometimes, as you are typing code in a Code window, Visual Basic will warn you immediately of a syntax error. At other times an error message will appear only after you attempt to run your program. In the steps that follow, you will purposely misspell a property name in order to generate such an error.

To trigger an error message:

1 Double-click cmdGreeting to open its Code window.

2 Edit the line of code within the subroutine by typing `lblHello.Captain = "Hello, world!"`
Notice that the Caption property has been misspelled as *Captain*.

3 Close the Code window and run the program.
A dialog box appears, displaying the message *Property 'Captain' not found.*

4 Select OK.
You are returned to the Visual Basic IDE. The Code window for cmdGreeting opens and displays the portion of your program where the error occurred.

5 Change the word *Captain* back to *Caption.*
6 Close the Code window, and run the program again to ensure that you corrected the error.

The error messages that Visual Basic generates will usually point you to the exact error that was made. In the above example, the message indicated that Captain was not a valid property name. It is easy to misspell property and variable names while coding, and many of the syntax errors that you cause will be due to spelling.

GETTING USER INPUT WITH A TEXT BOX

Next, you will add a **text box** that allows the user to input his or her name. A text box is a Visual Basic control that can display text. Unlike the Label control, however, the text in a Text Box control can be changed by the user. A Label control wouldn't be appropriate here because user input is needed.

> **Reminder** You use a Text Box control when you want the user to be able to edit, or change, text. For this reason a text box is sometimes referred to as an edit box. When the output text is designed to be unaffected by the user's actions, use a Label control. Labels are for output only.

 To add a Text Box control to your program:

 1 Select the Text Box tool, as shown in Figure 2.10.

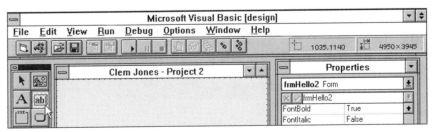

Figure 2.10

2 Trace a text box beneath the lblHello control, as shown in Figure 2.11.

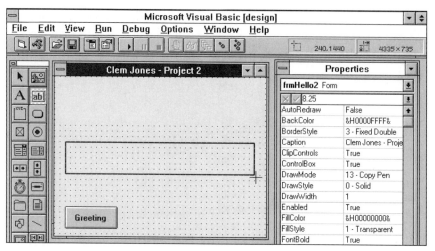

Figure 2.11

3 Make sure the text box is selected, double-click the **Name** property, and then type **txtInputName**

The text that appears within a text box is not called the Caption property but rather the Text property. The distinction is made because text in a text box can be changed by the user. Text that cannot be changed by the user is called a caption in Visual Basic. Initially, you will not want any default text appearing in the Text Box control.

> **Reminder** The text in a Text Box control is set with the Text property. Text in a Label control is set with the Caption property.

To change the default text in the Text Box control:

1 Change the **Text** property so that it is blank by backspacing over *Text1*.
You must edit the text for the text box in the Settings box on the Properties window, *not* directly in the text box on the form.

2 Change the **FontName** property to **Arial** and the **FontSize** property to **18** points.

3 Run the program.
You can click the text box to select it, and a ***text insertion bar*** will appear. The text insertion bar allows user-entered text to appear in the text box.

4 Stop the program.

> **Tip** You may notice a sizable delay when you first begin to enter text in any Windows program, including the ones you develop with Visual Basic. This is primarily due to font rendering time; subsequent use of the font during that particular Windows session will not have this delay.

In the previous steps the text insertion bar did not appear in the text box at first because the Greeting button has the initial ***focus***. Focus is a property that determines which object is the current, or selected, object.

That is, the focus indicates where action will take place. When a text box has the focus, the text insertion bar is present, and any text that is typed by the user will appear within the text box. It would make more sense if the text box had the initial focus. You will change this in the upcoming section.

CHANGING THE TABINDEX PROPERTY

The TabIndex property determines which control on a form has the initial focus and in which order the various controls get the focus as it is changed. The name TabIndex refers to the traditional Windows convention of using the (TAB) key to switch the focus from one control to another.

To change the TabIndex property:

1 Select txtInputName.

2 Change the **TabIndex** property to **0** (zero).

3 Run the program.

Now the text box has the initial focus, and the text insertion bar is visible when the program is first run.

4 Type your name in the text box, and click the Greeting button. The screen will look similar to Figure 2.12, with your name replacing *Clem Jones*.

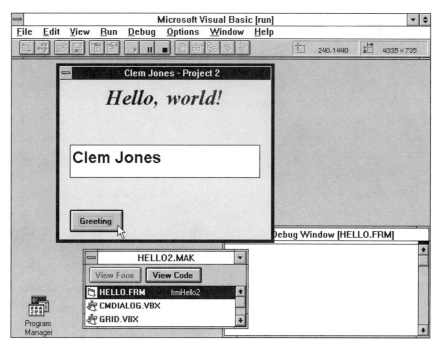

Figure 2.12

Notice that lblHello still displays *Hello, world!* This occurs because you have not yet changed the code for the Greeting button to make use of the text the user types in.

5 Stop the program.

WRITING CODE TO ACCESS THE TEXT PROPERTY

You will recall that when the user chooses the Greeting command button, a greeting message will appear in lblHello. You will need to write code in cmdGreeting's click event procedure to accomplish this.

To write code for the Text property:

1 Double-click cmdGreeting to open the Code window for that object.

2 Change the line that displays the greeting by typing:
`lblHello.Caption = "Hello, " & txtInputName.Text & "!"`

The screen should resemble Figure 2.13. The ampersand (&) means to *concatenate,* or attach, text strings. The txtInputName.Text term refers to the Text property of the txtInputName control. This line of code will print the word *Hello* followed by a comma, a space, the text that is input by the user in the Text Box control, and an exclamation point.

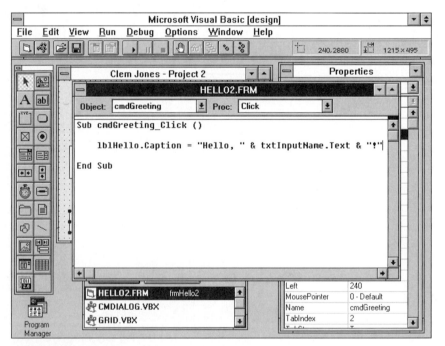

Figure 2.13

3 Close the Code Window, and run the program.

4 Type your first name in the text box, and click the Greeting button. Your name should now appear as part of the greeting message at the top of the window.

5 Stop the program.

In the following steps you will experiment with a special condition: What happens when the user clicks the Greeting button without having typed anything in the text box?

To test using the Greeting button without entering text:

1 Run the program again, and immediately click the Greeting button. As shown in Figure 2.14, the message *Hello, !* appears.

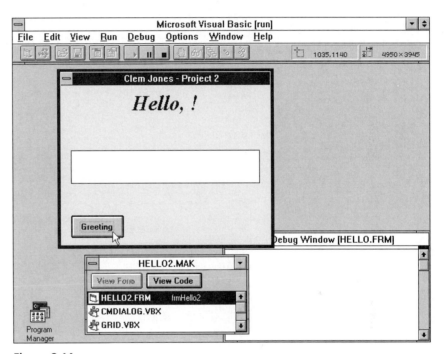

Figure 2.14

2 Stop the program.

The *Hello, !* message is inappropriate: The Greeting button should not be enabled unless there is some text typed in the text box. When the program initially loads, the Greeting button should be disabled, and it should remain so until a change event occurs in the text box.

This is a good example of a logic error: The program runs without any syntax errors, but it does not conform to your specifications. Sometimes it is difficult to find these types of errors when you program. Remember to exhaustively test your programs, trying out various operations that users would typically not try. These operations are often the source of errors because the programmer does not consider them.

ENABLING AND DISABLING CONTROLS

The Command button control has a property called Enabled. The Enabled property determines the user's access to that control. In fact, most controls have an Enabled property. In this program you want the cmdGreeting button to be *disabled* until the user inputs his or her name. In the following steps you will first disable the cmdGreeting button. Then you will change the Text Box control so it will enable cmdGreeting whenever a change event occurs. A **change event** for a text box occurs when text is typed by the user. If you leave out this step, cmdGreeting will never work!

To disable cmdGreeting's Enabled property and enable cmdGreeting from txtInputName:

1 Select the cmdGreeting button, and double-click the Enabled property to change it from True to False.

2 Select the txtInputName control, and double-click it to open the Code window.

3 In the Code window, make sure that the object is txtInputName and the procedure is Change.

4 Type `cmdGreeting.Enabled = True` within the subroutine, as shown in Figure 2.15.

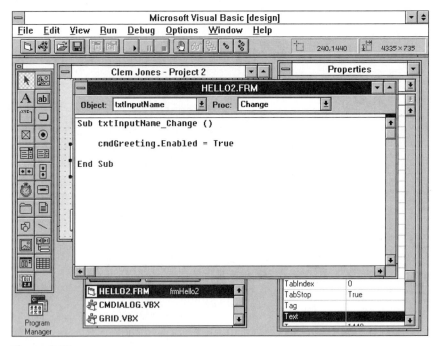

Figure 2.15

5 Close the Code window, and run the program.
As shown in Figure 2.16, cmdGreeting is initially disabled: The button's caption is dimmed.

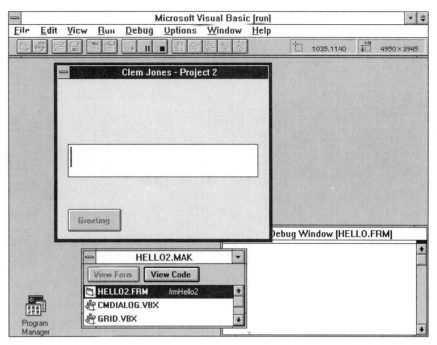

Figure 2.16

6 Type your name.
Note that as soon as you begin to type in the text box, cmdGreeting becomes enabled.

7 Click cmdGreeting.

8 Stop the program.

ADDING AN INSTRUCTION LABEL

In keeping with the user-friendly nature of Windows, your program should include a one-line prompt for the user to input his or her name below the text box. A Label control will fit the bill nicely because the text you will place there doesn't need to be changed by the user.

To add a small instruction label:

1 Add an instruction Label control, the same width as the Text Box control, centered under the text box, as shown in Figure 2.17.

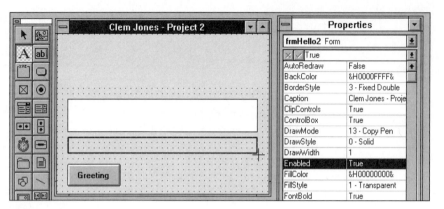

Figure 2.17

2 Double-click the **Name** property and type `lblInstruction`

3 Change the **BackColor** property to match the form BackColor property.

4 Set the **Alignment** property to **2-Center**.

5 Double-click the **Caption** property and type `Please type your name above`
The instruction label should resemble Figure 2.18.

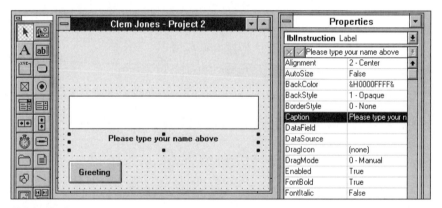

Figure 2.18

If you'd like, you can run the program now to see how the instruction label affects your program.

ADDING THE CLEAR BUTTON

You will now add a button to **clear** the txtInputName text box and the lblHello greeting label. In other words, when the user presses this button, it will erase any text that the user had placed in txtInputName. The button should also disable cmdGreeting, as well as itself, since it makes no sense to have either button enabled if there is no text in the text box.

To create the Clear command button:

1 Create a command button by double-clicking the Command Button icon on the Toolbox, and position the button to the right of the Greeting button, in the bottom center of the form.

2 Double-click the **Caption** property and type **Clear**

3 Double-click the **Name** property and type **cmdClear**

4 Double-click the **Enabled** property and set it to **False.**
This will cause the button to be initially disabled when the program is first run by the user. The Clear button should resemble Figure 2.19.

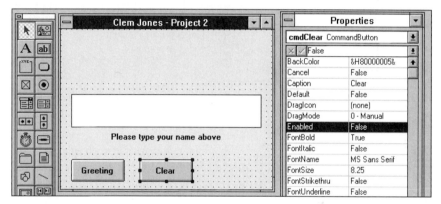

Figure 2.19

A change event in the text box will enable cmdClear.

To create a change event in the text box:

1 Select txtInputName, and double-click to open the Code window.

2 Type another line of code: **cmdClear.Enabled = True**
The screen should resemble Figure 2.20.

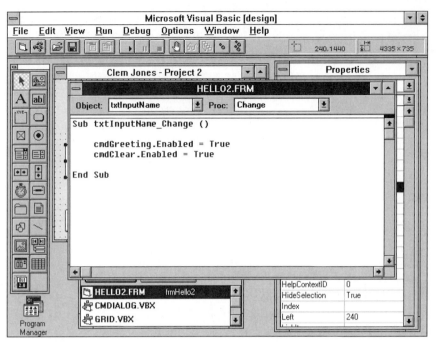

Figure 2.20

3 Close the Code window.

The Clear command itself also requires code. When it is clicked by the user, it should clear the text box and greeting label, and disable itself and the Greeting command button.

To add code to cmdClear:

1 Double-click cmdClear to open the Code window.

2 Enter the following lines of code, as shown in Figure 2.21. In Visual Basic code a pair of quotation marks signifies a blank (empty) string.

```
lblHello.Caption = ""

txtInputName.Text = ""

cmdGreeting.Enabled = False

cmdClear.Enabled = False
```

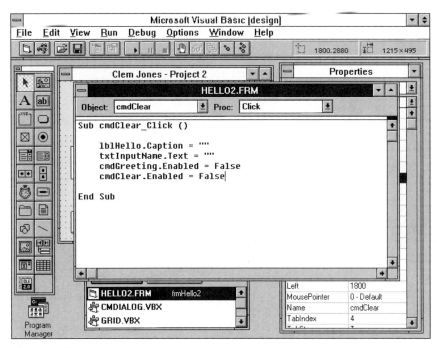

Figure 2.21

 Close the Code window, and run the program.

 Type your name in the text box, and then test the Greeting button and Clear button.

 Stop the program.

EXIT If necessary, you can save your work, exit Visual Basic, and continue this project later.

FINDING A SUBTLE LOGIC ERROR

The program, as it stands now, appears to work fine. But does it really? Remember that logic errors can be very subtle. Follow the next steps carefully: They will reveal a bug in the program.

To find the bug in the program:

 Run the program.

 Type a few characters into the text box.

 Backspace over the characters until the text box is empty.

 Click the Greeting button.
As shown in Figure 2.22, the greeting message *Hello, !* appears. This is inappropriate.

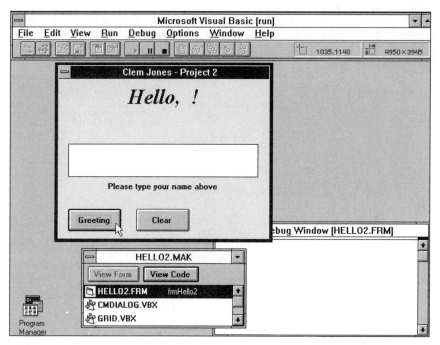

Figure 2.22

5 Stop the program.

USING THE IF-THEN-ELSE STATEMENT

The program is currently written so that any change in the txtInputName text box will enable the Greeting and Clear buttons. Unfortunately, this means that even if the user backspaces over the text in the box until it is empty, the two command buttons will still be enabled. It would be better if the program could determine whether the Text property of txtInputName was blank, and enable the two command buttons only if actual text was present.

The *If-Then-Else statement* is ideally suited to perform this kind of test. The If-Then-Else statement allows your program to execute certain lines of code, based on whether a certain condition is true. If the condition is true, the Then part of the statement is run. If the condition is false, the Else part is run.

In your program you need to check whether the txtInputName caption is blank. If it is blank, then the Greeting and Clear buttons should be disabled. If it is not blank, which is the Else part, then the Greeting and Clear buttons should be enabled.

Consider the pseudocode representation of these concepts:

```
If the Text property of txtInputName is blank Then
  Disable the Greeting and Clear buttons
Else
  Enable the Greeting and Clear buttons
End If
```

Because Visual Basic uses English-like syntax, the pseudocode will be fairly close to the actual code you need to write.

To modify the change event procedure code for txtInputName:

1 Select the txtInputName control.

2 Double-click the control to open the Code window.

3 Modify the code within the subroutine so that it looks like the following. Try to preserve the indenting style so that the subroutine is easy to read. Indents are made by pressing the (TAB) key, much as you would in any text editor or word processor.

```
If txtInputName.Text = "" Then
    cmdGreeting.Enabled = False
    cmdClear.Enabled = False
Else
    cmdGreeting.Enabled = True
    cmdClear.Enabled = True
End If
```

> **Tip** Visual Basic does not force you to follow any particular indenting style. However, program listings are much easier to read if they are indented logically.

4 Close the Code window.

5 Run the program.

6 Type your name in the text box.

7 Click the Clear button to test the code you have just entered.

8 Stop the program.

ADDING A CLOSE BUTTON

Forcing the user to use the Control-menu box to end the program isn't exactly a user-friendly feature. Considering that you have created command buttons to display the greeting and clear it, it makes sense to add a button that can be used to close the window and end the program. This will make your program more accessible: A Close button provides a convenient, one-click method to end the program. In addition, the Visual Basic code for the Close button will be the easiest you ever write.

The process of ending, or exiting, a Visual Basic program is handled by the **End statement.** While End is not required to terminate a Visual Basic program, it is a good idea to always include an End statement somewhere in your program code. Using End will clear the form and all variables from memory.

To create a Close button:

1 Double-click the command button icon on the Toolbox.

2 Type **Close** as the new command button **Caption** property and **cmdClose** as its **Name** property.

3 Position the Close button in the lower-right corner of frmHello2, as shown in Figure 2.23.

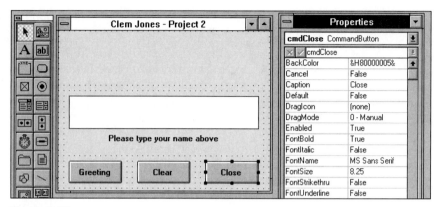

Figure 2.23

4 Double-click cmdClose to open its Code window.

5 Add the following short line of code within the subroutine:
End

6 Close the Code window, and run the program.

7 Enter your name, and click the Greeting button.

8 Click the Clear button.

Notice that the Clear button cleared the controls, but the focus was advanced to the next enabled control: the Close button. It would make better sense if the focus returned to the txtInputName text box instead.

To return focus to txtInputName after the Clear button is pressed:

1 Stop the program by using the Close button.

2 Select the Clear button, and double-click to open the Code window.

3 Add a final line of code to cmdClear_Click: `txtInputName.SetFocus`
The screen should resemble Figure 2.24.

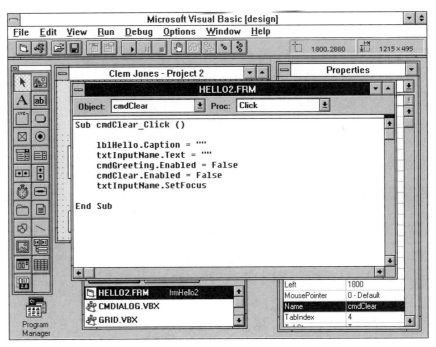

Figure 2.24

SetFocus is a ***method*** that is used to change the focus in your program. A method is similar in meaning to a property except that a method is essentially a built-in procedure or action. A property is assigned a value, like true or false, whereas a method is called, like a procedure, by attaching the method name to an object using a convention not unlike *objectName.PropertyName*.

> **Tip** Properties are specific attributes of an object. Methods are specific actions done to an object. Though they are conceptually different, the syntax for using properties and methods is the same.

Notice that you did not enter *SetFocus = True*. The syntax for the SetFocus method is *object.SetFocus*, where *object* is a form or control. In this case, the object is the txtInputName text box, so *txtInputName.SetFocus* sets the focus to txtInputName.

When SetFocus is encountered while the program is running, the user input, or focus, is directed to the specified form or control. In other words, the cursor is placed in the specified object. You are setting the focus to txtInputName, redirecting it from cmdClose, which would be the next focus normally.

To test the SetFocus method:

1 Close the Code window.

2 Run the program, paying attention to where the focus is set after different events.

3 Stop the program.

4 Save the file.

THE NEXT STEP

In this project you created Visual Basic code for the first time. In the next project you will develop more advanced code that will perform calculations. You will create a new form that will provide the backdrop for an electricity calculator.

This concludes Project 2. You can either exit Visual Basic now or go on to work the Study Questions, Review Exercises, and Assignments.

SUMMARY AND EXERCISES

Summary

- To create a truly useful Visual Basic program, you will need to write program code.
- A command button provides the user with an obvious way to cause an action to occur.
- An event procedure is a block of code, or subroutine, that executes in response to an event.
- A Text Box control displays text that can be changed by the user.
- The TabIndex property determines which control on a form gets the initial focus and is named for the Windows method of changing focus by using the (TAB) key.
- Logic errors are often found in programs and can be very subtle. Only through extensive testing can you find all errors.
- You use the If-Then-Else statement to make a decision and then branch to certain lines of code based on the outcome of that decision.
- The End command ends a Visual Basic program.

Key Terms and Operations

Key Terms
call
change event
clear
click event procedure
click procedure
Code window
command button
concatenate
End statement
focus
event procedure
If-Then-Else statement

method
proc
subroutine
text box
text insertion bar

Operations
Reuse a previous form
Use the Code window
Write event procedures
Find logic errors
Make decisions with an If-Then-Else statement

Study Questions

Multiple Choice

1. When you want the user to trigger an event, which control should you use?
   a. Text Box
   b. Label
   c. Command Button
   d. Control-Menu Box
   e. Yes Box

2. Which of the following will trigger an event procedure?
   a. The user selects the Quit command button.
   b. The user clicks on a blank area of the form.
   c. The user clicks the left mouse button.
   d. The user enters text in a text box.
   e. All of the above.

3. An event procedure is
   a. an endless loop.
   b. a subroutine.
   c. possible only in QuickBasic.
   d. coded in the Properties window.
   e. used in flowcharting only.

4. How is a text box different from a Label control?
   a. The text box does not allow the user to change the text it displays.
   b. The text box can be moved by the user.
   c. The text box is faster than the Label control.
   d. The text box is used in event procedures.
   e. The text box allows the user to change the text it displays.

5. Which of the following is used to make decisions?
   a. the If-Than-Else statement
   b. the Else-If-Then statement
   c. the If-Then-Else statement
   d. the If-Else statement
   e. None of the above.

6. Which of the following is the command used to terminate a Visual Basic program?
   a. Stop
   b. Quit
   c. End
   d. Terminate
   e. Else

7. A method is similar to a
   a. property.
   b. procedure.
   c. project.
   d. Text Box control.
   e. subroutine.

8. In Visual Basic code, changing the caption of the label named lblFooBar to *the Visual Basic Way* would require the syntax
   a. lblFooBar.SetCaption = "the Visual Basic Way"
   b. lblFooBar.SetTitle = "the Visual Basic Way"

   c. lblFooBar.Caption = "the Visual Basic Way"
   d. lblFooBar.CaptionSet. "the Visual Basic Way"
   e. Caption.lblFooBar = "the Visual Basic Way"

9. What symbol is used to indicate concatenation?
   a. *
   b. #
   c. &
   d. %
   e. @

10. To disable a command button named cmdPushMe, which syntax applies?
   a. cmdPushMe.Enabled = True
   b. cmdPushMe.Disabled = True
   c. cmdPushMe.Enabled = False
   d. cmdPushMe.Disable
   e. cmdPushMe.Enabled = Yes

Short Answer

1. What prefix do you use to name a Command button?

2. When is a Click Event procedure triggered?

3. How do you access the Code window?

4. How did the TabIndex property get its name?

5. Which control would you use to display text that shouldn't be changed by the user?

6. How do you access the Code window for a control?

7. The test within an If-Then-Else statement can result in what alternatives?

8. In the Hungarian naming convention, what is the prefix for a text box?

9. How is a method similar to a property? How is it different?

10. Describe how to change the focus in your program?

For Discussion

1. Logic errors can be very subtle. Describe the best method to ensure that you have eliminated all possible logic errors.

2. Describe how to create a command button.

3. Describe when to use a Label control instead of a Text Box control.

4. Describe the methods that can be used to terminate a Visual Basic program.

5. Why would you want to disable a control, thus removing the user's access to that control?

Review Exercises

Writing Pseudocode for Password Protection

Write pseudocode for a program that will prompt the user to enter a password. If the correct password is entered, the program should display a message indicating so. If the password is entered incorrectly, another message will be displayed. The program should have a label to prompt the user, a command button to allow the user to finish input, and a text box to display the confirmation message.

Writing Pseudocode for Font Display

Write pseudocode for a program that will prompt the user to enter some text and a font. The entered text will then be displayed on the form in that point size. This program will require two text boxes: one for the text and one for the point size. This also requires a Label control to display the text in the new point size.

Assignments

Designing a Password Window

Using the skills you developed with this project and the pseudocode you designed in the first review exercise in this project as a guide, design a window that presents the user with a password entry text, as shown in Figure 2.25.

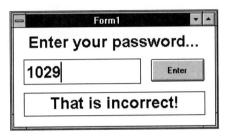

Figure 2.25

Designing a Font Display Dialog Box

Design the font display window that you wrote pseudocode for in the second review exercise in this project. The window should resemble Figure 2.26.

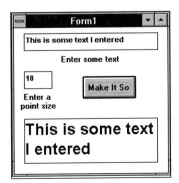

Figure 2.26

PROJECT 3: PERFORMING CALCULATIONS WITH VISUAL BASIC

Objectives

After completing this project, you should be able to:

▶ Declare variables and constants

▶ Perform simple calculations

▶ Use Visual Basic functions

▶ Use the assignment operator (=) to assign values to variables

▶ Format output with the Format function

▶ Designate the Startup form

CASE STUDY: ESTIMATING AN ELECTRIC BILL

Electric power companies perform complex calculations to determine the billing for each customer based on energy consumption, time of consumption, and season. In the warmer climates of sunbelt states like Arizona, energy is more expensive in the summer months, as the load on power generators increases. Most people don't really understand how their electric bills are determined and why electricity is more expensive on certain days, hours, and times of the year.

While you might be hard-pressed to sympathize with the computations that utility companies make on a daily basis, an exploration of the process will garner an understanding of simple systems analysis and introduce some Visual Basic programming techniques at the same time.

Designing the Solution

This project involves writing a program that could be used by customer service representatives (CSRs) of an electric utility company to estimate an electric bill quickly. This type of customized calculator could be running on systems used by telephone CSRs or on the notebook computers of energy conservation representatives in the field. When the user types in a number of kilowatt-hours used, the cost is shown, taking into account not only the basic cost per kilowatt-hour but also a fuel cost adjustment factor and the tax rate.

The program you will develop for this project will provide the basis for the following two projects. These upcoming projects will improve the program and make it more powerful and versatile.

The specifications for this project are as follows:

- The program should be an easy-to-use electricity bill calculator.
- The user should be able to type in the number of kilowatt-hours consumed by a residential customer and find out the cost of such usage.
- The program should be designed for computing electricity cost for the summer billing months only (June through September).
- The summer rate is $0.0942 per kilowatt hour, regardless of the number of kilowatt hours used.
- The cost is reduced by a fuel factor of $0.001403 per kilowatt-hour used.
- Taxes are 8.20 percent.

The program will follow these steps:

- Calculate a raw cost by multiplying the number of kilowatt-hours used by the rate, $0.0942.
- Subtract the fuel factor adjustment, which is the number of kilowatt-hours used multiplied by the fuel factor, $0.001403.
- Multiply by a tax multiplier, 1.082 (1 + tax rate), to arrive at the total cost.

Using the OPE Flowchart

Figure 3.1 shows the flowchart for the program. You will use the flowchart, along with the specifications, to set up the basic form and controls. You should assign properties to each object as shown in the flowchart.

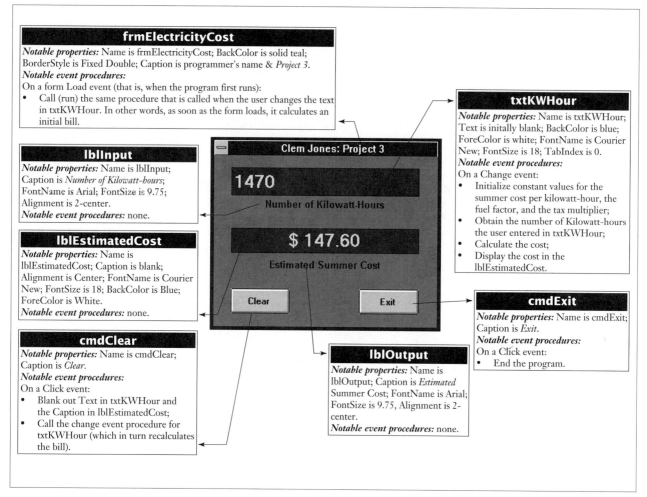

Figure 3.1

 To begin developing the new program:

1 Create the form and its controls following the specifications and the flowchart. Make sure you assign all properties as indicated and name each object correctly, because the code you will be writing depends on these.

2 Save the form as ELECTRIC.FRM and the project as ELECTRIC.MAK.

STORING VALUES IN CONSTANTS AND VARIABLES

When programming, you will often want to store values that are reused throughout the course of your program. Like other programming languages, Visual Basic uses constants and variables to hold these values.

Constants are used to hold values that will not change for the "life" of the program. A constant is fixed, set in stone. Typical constants would include the value of pi and the number of days in a week. These numbers will not change, so a constant would be the obvious choice.

Variables are used to hold values that can be changed while the program is running. A variable has a ***name,*** which is the word you use to access the variable in your code, and a ***data type,*** which describes the category of data that the variable can contain.

The data type given to a variable will depend on what the variable will be used for. Whole numbers, that is numbers without a decimal point, are typically of type ***Integer.*** Integers are useful for counting and other computations with no decimal precision involved. There are various other numerical data types, as well as a data type for text called ***String.***

Declaring Constants and Variables

Advanced programming languages like Pascal force you to ***declare*** constants and variables before they are used in a program. A declaration tells the compiler to set aside memory for the variable or constant. In fact, this is why variables and constants have data types in the first place: Different data types have different memory storage requirements.

Visual Basic, unfortunately, does not *require* you to declare variables. When a computation occurs, there is no doubt what type of value the result will have when type declaration is enforced. In Visual Basic's defense, most implementations of BASIC have not supported forced type declaration. However, there is a switch in the Visual Basic Environment Options dialog box that will turn this feature on. It is very important that you do so.

To enable the declaration-required feature:

1 Choose **Options** and then **Environment**.
The Environment Options dialog box appears.

2 Select the option titled **Require Variable Declaration,** and change this option to **Yes** if necessary.

3 Select **OK** to close the dialog box.

> **Reminder** Always enable the Require Variable Declaration option in the Environment Options dialog box.

Variables are declared in your code using the ***Dim statement.*** Dim, short for Dimension, is used in conjunction with the word *As* to declare variables, as in the following statements:

```
Dim Count As Integer
Dim Quote As String
```

The first example reserves a memory storage location of type Integer; the name you are giving it is Count.

Constants are declared by using the ***Const statement*** followed by an assignment operator (=) and the constant name. Examples of valid constants include the following:

```
Const Pi = 3.14
Const NumYearDays = 365
```

Naming Constants and Variables

Constant and Variable names are given by the programmer and should be descriptive. In early versions of BASIC, these names could only be a letter or two long, and variables like A1, NM, and X were common. Not very descriptive, are they? Visual Basic allows for long, descriptive names, so ThisIsMyVariableName is not out of the question.

Visual Basic has only a few general rules for naming constants and variables. A constant or variable

- Must begin with a letter.
- Must contain only letters, numbers, and the underscore (_) character. Punctuation and spaces are not allowed.
- Must be 40 or fewer characters in length.
- Cannot be a **reserved word**. A reserved word is a word that is part of the Visual Basic language. For example, you cannot use the words *If*, *Then*, and *Else* as variable or constant names.

> ***Tip*** As with controls, there are various naming conventions for variable names, including Hungarian notation. The variable names you will be creating here, however, will not include the data type prefix. Sometimes it is more advantageous to use descriptive names without the prefix. The variable CityName is as understandable as sCityName, for example. You should be aware, though, that different programmers use different naming styles. You should use a naming convention that makes sense to you or to the person who assigned the programming project you are working on.

PERFORMING CALCULATIONS

Visual Basic allows you to carry out mathematical operations like addition, subtraction, multiplication, and division. Some of the symbols that Visual Basic uses to signify arithmetic operators may seem a little strange if you have never used a computer programming language before, although they will be familiar to Excel users.

The following table describes the arithmetic operators:

Operator	Operation
+	Addition
–	Subtraction
*	Multiplication
^	Exponentiation
/	Floating point division
\	Integer division (no remainder is given)
Mod	Modulus (the remainder from an integer division)

Tip Don't confuse the / and \ operators. They give totally different results. If you perform the operation 5.25 / .27 the result would be 4.1338526771654. Using the \ operator, the answer would be 5.

Certain rules apply to performing arithmetic in Visual Basic. When two values occur in an arithmetic expression, each value is called an *operand*. If you perform an operation on two numbers with different data types, the result is given the data type of the operand with the wider range. For example, Integers have a range of −32,768 to 32,767, and Longs have a range of −2,147,483,648 to 2,147,483,647. Dividing a Long by an Integer results in a Long. A variable that is declared as a Long can be much larger than a number that is declared as an Integer.

Integer division is used to truncate the remainder. If the remainder needs to be used elsewhere, a Modulus operation to the same numbers will derive that value:

```
Dim TotalDays As Integer
Dim Weeks As Integer
Dim DaysLeftOver As Integer

TotalDays = 93
Weeks = TotalDays \ 7          ‘ this will output 13 if printed
DaysLeftOver = TotalDays Mod 7 ‘ this will output 2 if printed
```

EXIT If necessary, you can save your work, exit Visual Basic, and continue this project later.

Developing Code to Perform Calculations

The electricity cost should be calculated any time a change is made (information is entered or modified) to the txtKWHour text box.

 ### To add code to txtKWHour:

1 Select the txtKWHour control, and double-click to open its Code window.

2 Enter code for the Change event procedure of txtKWHour.

```
Dim Cost As Single
Dim KWHours As Single
Const SummerCostPerKWHour = .0942
Const FuelFactor = .001403
Const TaxMultiplier = 1.082

KWHours = Val(txtKWHour.Text)

Cost = KWHours * SummerCostPerKWHour
Cost = Cost - KWHours * FuelFactor
Cost = Cost * TaxMultiplier
lblEstimatedCost.Caption = Format(Cost, “$ ##,##0.00”)
```

The screen should resemble Figure 3.2.

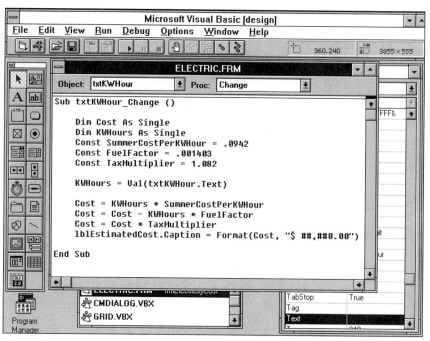

Figure 3.2

Look at the first few lines of code in txtKWHour_Change. The line

```
Dim Cost As Single
```

means that the programmer wants to create a variable called Cost that is designed to hold *single-precision floating point numbers,* called a *Single* for short. A Single is a number that can have digits to the right of the decimal point, like 3.14. Once Cost is declared, it can be used to hold the results of calculations.

> **Tip** You can use a data type called Currency to hold numbers that represent monetary values, but you will be using variables of type Single instead because these variables will be used in computations with other Single values. This will prevent any Currency-to-Single conversion problems.

It is easy to see why constants are used instead of "hard coding" the values they represent. The following is an example of what the code listed in txtKWHour would look like without named constants:

```
Cost = KWHours * .0942
Cost = Cost - KWHours * .001403
Cost = Cost * 1.082
```

The presence of so many hard-coded numbers makes the program more difficult to understand and to maintain. What if the fuel factor changed? In a longer program you would have to search through all of the code, looking for each .001403 so you could change it to the new value. Using a single named constant means that future changes will be easy: You will only need to change one number.

The difficulty understanding and working with hard-coded constants has led to a pejorative term for them: *magic numbers.* After a program has been in use for a few years and the original programmer has moved on to another job, magic numbers are especially fun to decipher for the poor person whose job it is to maintain the program.

The TaxMultiplier constant was arrived at in this way: An easy method to calculate an after-tax total bill is to multiply the amount by 1 plus the tax rate.

USING FUNCTIONS

A *function* is a special type of procedure that *returns* (sends back) a value. This means that a function can be used on the right side of the equal sign in a Visual Basic statement. There are many functions built into the Visual Basic language that you can use. Also, you can write your own functions, similar in manner to writing event procedures. A function takes *arguments,* which are the input for the function, and returns a value, which is the output. Because a function returns a value, it can be used in larger expressions.

Functions differ from procedures in a few ways:

- Functions have a data type, just like a variable. This is the type of the return value of the function.
- If you are writing your own function, you return a value by assigning it to the function name. When the function returns the value, this value can be used as part of an expression.

Consider the following hypothetical function:

```
Function MySum (Number1, Number2) As Single
  MySum = Number1 + Number2
End Function
```

The function, named MySum, accepts two arguments, Number1 and Number2. It assigns the sum of the two arguments to the function name in the body of the function. This is the value that is returned. Because the data type given to the function is a Single, the returned value is also a Single.

In another part of the program, you could then call the MySum function, as in the following code example:

```
Total = MySum(Number1, Number2)
```

Functions are useful because the programmer usually doesn't need to know *how* a function works, just the arguments that are required and the return type. You will begin using some of Visual Basic's built-in functions in upcoming sections, despite the fact that you will not have a clear idea of how they work. This distinction is important; how the function works is irrelevant. You only need to know what to send it and what it will return.

Using the Val Function

Consider the line

```
KWHours = Val(txtKWHour.Text)
```

Val is a function that returns the numeric value of a string of characters. A function is like a black box: Something goes in the box and it returns a value. In this case the something going into the Val function box is the text in the Text property of txtKWHour. Input text is by default a string of characters, not a numerical expression. The purpose of the Val function is to return the numeric value of that string, so the result it returns is just that: a numeric value.

Recall that txtKWHour is the text input box where the user types the number of kilowatt-hours used. The value extracted by Val is then placed in the variable called KWHours, which was declared at the top of the procedure.

Using the Assignment Operator (=)

The equal sign (=) does not have the same meaning in Visual Basic as an equal sign in a mathematical equation. In algebra an equal sign asserts that the items on each side of the equal sign are the same. In Visual Basic the equal sign, or *assignment operator,* usually means "calculate the value of whatever instructions are on the right side of the equal sign, and then store that value in the variable named on the left side of the equal sign." For example, the line

```
Cost = KWHours * SummerCostPerKWHour
```

means to multiply the number of kilowatt-hours used by the summer rate (a constant declared at the top of the procedure) and store the result in the variable Cost.

The line

```
Cost = Cost - Cost * FuelFactor
```

calculates the fuel factor discount and subtracts it from the cost, assigning the result into the variable Cost. Recall that FuelFactor is a constant declared at the top of the procedure. As in Excel, multiplication has higher priority than subtraction, so the multiplication portion of this statement is calculated first: The statement has the same meaning as Cost = Cost - (Cost * FuelFactor).

The line

```
Cost = Cost * TaxMultiplier
```

uses the TaxMultiplier constant to compute the final cost.

Formatting Output

Visual Basic uses the *Format function* to format, or *punctuate*, the output of a number, date, time, or string. Consider the line:

```
lblEstimatedCost.Caption = Format(Cost, "$ ##,##0.00")
```

The first part looks simple enough. You are trying to place the value of the Cost variable in the caption for lblEstimatedCost. Format is a function, and, like Val, will return a value. This particular function requires *two* arguments: the variable you want formatted and the formatting you want done to it. These objects are what appear inside the parentheses. In this case the value that this function returns is the value of the Cost variable, formatted the way that you specified.

The Format function uses a variety of special symbols to determine how the displayed value will look, a particularly nice feature for report generation. In the ELECTRIC program you are specifying that the output include a dollar sign and a space, followed by the number. The number will include commas if it is over 999. Also, it will display two digits to the right of the decimal point. Numbers less than zero will still display a single zero to the left of the decimal point for clarity.

TESTING THE PROGRAM

The program has now been developed enough that it can be run and tested. You should constantly test the programs you create, to uncover possible syntax and logic errors.

To test the code you've written:

1 Run the program.
Note that there is no initial value displayed for the estimated cost. Though this value would only be 0 for summer rates, the specifications still call for an initial calculation.

2 Type the value of *1470* for the number of kilowatt-hours.
A resulting cost of $147.60 should be displayed, as shown in Figure 3.3. Note that the Clear and Exit buttons are not yet functional.

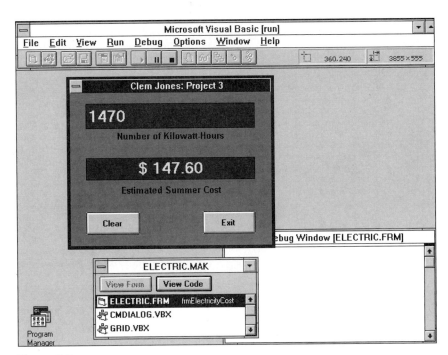

Figure 3.3

3 Stop the program.

Experimenting with Output Format

You can see the effect that Format has on output by simply removing it. This is only a temporary change, so you will need to find a way to temporarily change the txtKWHour Click procedure. Visual Basic has a statement called **Rem**, for remark, which can be used to disable the line you would like to skip temporarily. Rem, or its equivalent, the ' character, is good for adding explanatory lines to your programs:

```
Rem This Line is a comment only and will not be executed
' This is also a remark. The ' character can be used in place of Rem
```

To temporarily remove the formatted output:

1 Double-click txtKWHour to open its Code window.

2 Edit the line of code

```
lblEstimatedCost.Caption = Format(Cost, "$ ##,##0.00")
```

by typing

```
'lblEstimatedCost.Caption = Format(Cost, "$ ##,##0.00")
lblEstimatedCost.Caption = Cost
```

The screen should resemble Figure 3.4.

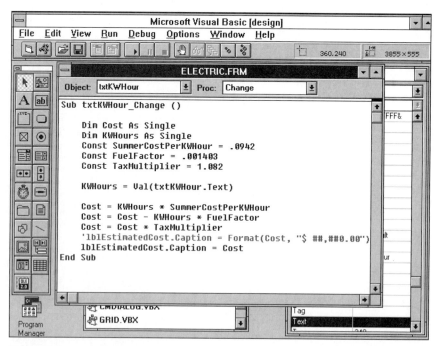

Figure 3.4

3 Run the program and enter various numbers, noting the output in lblEstimatedCost.

Figure 3.5 shows the effect of removing the format when the input is 1470.

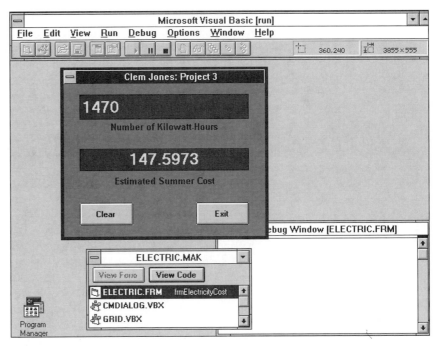

Figure 3.5

4 Stop the program.

You may want to experiment with the various predefined formats. When you are done, delete the remark character and the recently added line so that the program functions as before.

WRITING CODE THAT RUNS AS THE PROGRAM LOADS

Visual Basic allows you to specify which form in your program is the *Startup form.* The Startup form is the form that first loads when a user runs your program. Since this program has only one form, that form defaults to the Startup form.

In the steps that follow, you will write a short line of code that executes when frmElectricityCost loads. Because this form is the Startup form, the code will execute when the program is first run. This code will cause the txtKWHour_Change event procedure to be called.

Because the initial value in the text box is zero, the calculated summer cost will also be zero. In later projects this automatic initial calculation will be important because winter rates involve a minimum charge regardless of the amount of electricity used.

To enter code that will run when your program is first executed:

1 Select the form, and double-click to open the form's Code window.

2 Make sure that the object is Form and the event procedure is Load, and then type txtKWHour_Change within the subroutine.

The screen should resemble Figure 3.6. This line of code produces the same effect as the user actually changing the value in the KWHoursText input box. When this statement executes, it in effect generates a change event for the KWHourText control.

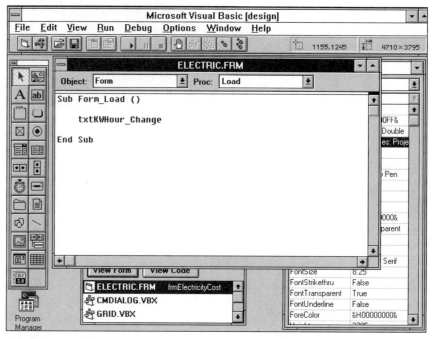

Figure 3.6

3 Close the Code window.

ADDING CODE TO THE CLEAR AND EXIT COMMAND BUTTONS

The Clear and Exit command buttons will need to have functionality added to their respective click event procedures.

To enter code for the Clear and Exit command buttons:

1 Select the Clear control, double-click to open its Code window, and type the following lines of code within the subroutine:

```
txtKWHour.Text = ""
lblEstimatedCost.Caption = ""
txtKWHour_Change
txtKWHour.SetFocus
```

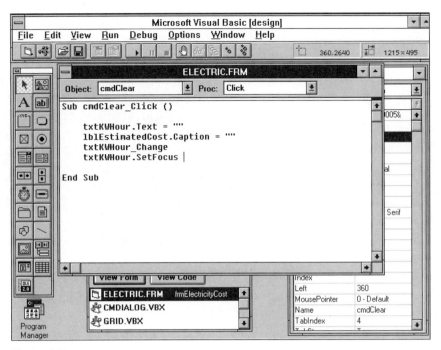

Figure 3.7

The screen should resemble Figure 3.7. This code should be self-explanatory to you now. Technically, the line that clears txtKWHour.Text will automatically trigger a change event for txtKWHour, so the lines that clear lblEstimatedCost.Caption and explicitly call txtKWHour_Change are not really necessary, though they make the programmer's intentions more obvious to other people who may later have to change the code.

2 Close the Code window.

3 Select the Exit control, double-click to open its Code window, type End within the subroutine, and then close the Code window.

4 Run and test the program, as shown in Figure 3.8, correcting any errors you discover.

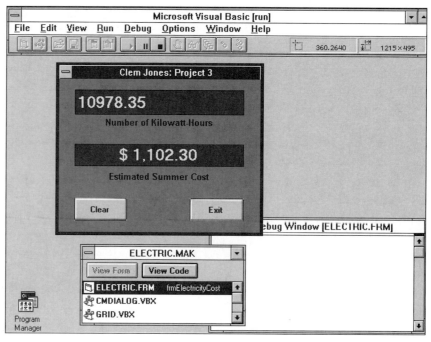

Figure 3.8

5 Save your project.

6 Make an executable version of your program.

THE NEXT STEP

Your investigation of electrical billing has just begun. In this project you have developed a simple calculator that determines the cost of electricity for the summer months only.

In the next project you will enhance the calculator to include the winter months and give the user the option of switching between the two. The winter calculations will also include a sliding rate scale, making that estimate a little more difficult.

This concludes Project 3. You can either exit Visual Basic or go on to work the Study Questions, Review Exercises, and Assignments.

SUMMARY AND EXERCISES

Summary

- Temporary values used in your program can be stored using variables and constants.
- A variable is used to store values that can change.
- Variables have a name and data type.
- The Dim statement is used to declare variables.
- Constants are declared with the Const statement.

- Single-precision floating point numbers are numbers that have digits to the right of the decimal point.
- The Val function accepts a string of characters and returns a numeric value.
- The Format function is used to format number, date, time, or string output.
- The Rem statement (or ' character) is used to add descriptive remarks to your program code.
- The Startup form is the form that loads when the program begins.

Key Terms and Operations

Key Terms

argument
assignment operator
Const statement
constant
data type
declare
Dim statement
Format function
function
Integer
magic number
name
operand
Rem statement

reserved word
return
Single
single-precision floating point number
Startup form
String
Val function
variable

Operations

Declare variables and constants
Format output
Perform calculations
Use functions

Study Questions

Multiple Choice

1. A variable is used to hold a value that
   a. can move.
   b. stays the same.
   c. changes.
   d. is never declared.
   e. is not typed.

2. A constant is used to hold a value that
   a. can move.
   b. stays the same.
   c. changes.
   d. is never declared.
   e. is not typed.

3. Variables and constants should always be
   a. numbers.
   b. letters.
   c. variant.
   d. easy to remember.
   e. declared.

4. Variables and constants have data types to
   a. confuse the programmer.
   b. satisfy the requirements for object-oriented programming.
   c. determine memory storage requirements.

    d. format output automatically.

    e. allow equations with nonnumerical values.

5. Dim is short for
   a. dementia.
   b. dimension.
   c. dim sum.
   d. low power consumption.
   e. outer dimension.

6. Which of the following symbols is used to denote integer division?
   a. /
   b. &
   c. (
   d. *
   e. \

7. One way that a function is different from a procedure is that a function
   a. cannot be written by the programmer.
   b. can return a value.
   c. does not accept an argument or arguments.
   d. is not typed.
   e. can be triggered by an event procedure.

8. The assignment operator uses which symbol?
   a. _
   b. ~
   c. =
   d. !=
   e. #

9. Which function is used to format output?
   a. Form
   b. TextDisplay
   c. Caption
   d. Format
   e. frmFormat

10. The Startup form is the form that
    a. opens when the program is first run.
    b. tells your program to begin.
    c. ends an event procedure.
    d. returns a value to the system.
    e. tells Windows that your program is ready to begin.

Short Answer

1. What is the difference between variables and constants?

2. Why do variables have a data type?

3. Are constants values that never change?

4. What statement is used to declare a variable?

5. Can you force Visual Basic to require variable declarations?

6. What is the statement used to declare a constant?

7. What is the difference between integer and floating point division?

8. Would Visual Basic allow you to name a variable Dim? Why or why not?

9. What is the Val function used for?

10. What is the equal sign (=) used for?

For Discussion

1. Visual Basic does not require you to declare variable types. Why should you do so anyway?

2. Describe the code used to multiply three numbers together.

3. Functions are really a specialized form of procedure. What makes a function different from a normal procedure?

4. Constants do have a type associated with their declaration. Why do you think this is so?

5. In algebra the expression X = X + 1 is always false. Can you make use of such a statement in Visual Basic? How/why?

Review Exercises

Writing a Simple Function

In Project 2 you used two functions: the Val function and the Format function. Use your recently developed skills to write a pseudocode function that accepts two numbers and returns the number that is larger numerically. Don't worry if the values are the same. Assume the function only works with Integer numbers. You will need to use an If-Then-Else decision loop to determine the larger number.

Writing the Pseudocode for an Addition Calculator

Develop the pseudocode for a calculator program that only adds numbers. There should be a Text Box control for input and a Label control to display the current total. A command button with the caption Add will be used to add the value in the text box to the current total. A Clear button will clear the values, and a Close button will end the program.

Assignments

Turning the Addition Calculator into a Program

Using the pseudocode from the second review exercise in this project and Figure 3.9 as a guide, develop the calculator into a running program.

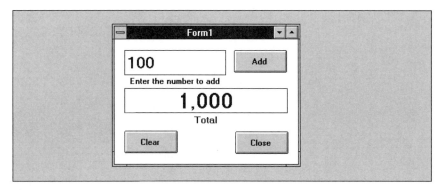

Figure 3.9

Expanding the Calculator

Expand the calculator from the first assignment to include a Subtract button, as shown in Figure 3.10. The button, when pressed, should subtract the value in the input text box from the total and display the new total.

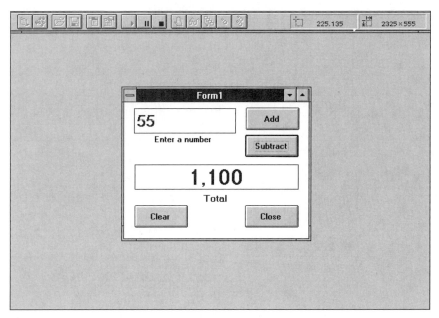

Figure 3.10

PROJECT 4: IMPROVING THE ENERGY COST CALCULATOR

Objectives

After completing this project, you should be able to:

▶ Group option buttons within a frame

▶ Add code to Option Button controls

▶ Add a horizontal scroll bar to receive input

▶ Use the Select Case statement

▶ Use a sliding scale to perform calculations

▶ Employ nested If-Then-Else statements

CASE STUDY: IMPROVING THE ELECTRICITY PROGRAM

As discussed in Project 3, energy consumption is more expensive in the winter for colder climates. Places like Arizona and Florida, however, increase their energy consumption in the summer when air conditioning units are running almost constantly. These increased loads cause higher prices as the capacity of utility companies is strained to meet demand. Utility companies usually employ a complex version of a sliding scale to determine pricing.

Designing the Solution

In this project you will enhance the electricity cost calculator you created in Project 3 so that it is able to use different rates for summer and winter. Summer costs will be calculated the same way as in Project 3. Winter usage will include a basic fee of $10.99 that will be charged regardless of the amount of electricity used. However, your program will now calculate total winter electricity costs using a sliding scale: The first 400 kilowatt-hours used will cost more per kilowatt-hour than the next 400, and so forth.

The specifications for this project are as follows:

■ The electricity cost calculator should be modified so that the user is presented with a pair of options labeled Summer and Winter. Calculation of electricity costs should depend on which option the user selects.

■ The visual style of the program should change (see the flowchart in Figure 4.1). A horizontal scroll bar should be added to allow the user to input the number of kilowatt-hours in a different manner.

■ Calculation of summer costs should be identical to Project 3.

- A sliding price scale will be used for computing winter electric costs. Calculation of winter costs will include a basic charge of $10.99, regardless of the number of kilowatt-hours used. Winter electric usage is then billed using the following rate scale: $0.0834 per kilowatt-hour for the first 400 kilowatt-hours used; $0.0635 per kilowatt-hour for 401 to 800 kilowatt-hours; and $0.0396 for 801 kilowatt-hours and above. Note that the marginal rate per kilowatt-hour decreases as the consumer uses more electricity.
- The fuel factor adjustment and taxes should be applied to the cost for both summer and winter.

Using the OPE Flowchart

Figure 4.1 shows the OPE flowchart for your new project. The new flowchart shows only those aspects of Project 3 that will change for the new project. Two *option buttons* are used so that the user can choose summer or winter rates. Option Button controls are used to display a choice of options that are *mutually exclusive*; that is, only one option can be selected at a time. It wouldn't make sense for winter and summer rates to be selected at the same time.

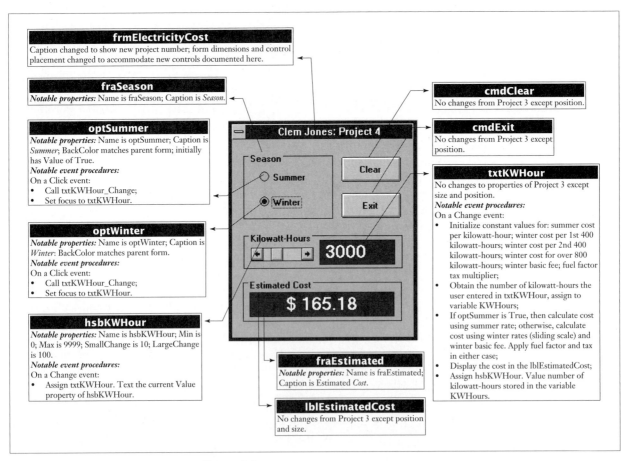

Figure 4.1

The first step in creating the new project is visually to redesign the form and its controls using the specifications and the flowchart shown in Figure 4.1. At this point don't worry about the Frame and Option Button controls; you will add them later. In the following steps you will rearrange the existing controls.

To modify the existing form:

1 Open the ELECTRIC project, and immediately save the form as ENERGY.FRM using Save File As.

2 Save the project as ENERGY.MAK

3 Edit the form's **Caption** property to show that it is Project 4.

4 Resize the form and place the existing controls, using Figure 4.1 as a guide.

5 Drag the cmdClear and cmdExit buttons to the upper-right corner of the form.

6 Delete lblInput and lblOutput by selecting them and pressing (DEL). The form should now resemble Figure 4.2.

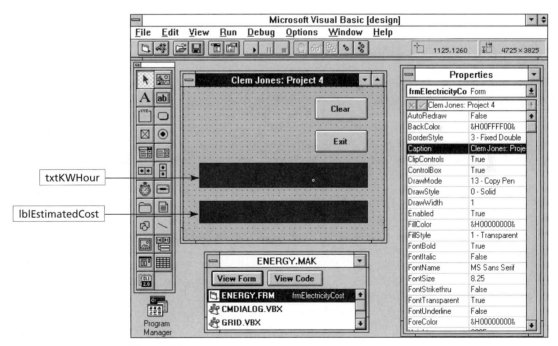

Figure 4.2

Tip Don't worry about precisely positioning the controls now. As more controls are added, their positions will probably need to change a bit anyway.

ADDING A FRAME CONTROL

As shown in Figure 4.1; the option buttons and labels are surrounded by a border that has a descriptive text caption. This border is called a ***Frame control***. The frame is used to create logical groups of related controls. For example, option buttons are often grouped in a frame. You will also be using frames to create borders around lblEstimatedCost and txtKWHour.

When you create a Frame control, you can place other controls, like option buttons, on top of the frame. This is an important distinction. The option buttons on the frame are *not* directly on the *form*. They are on the *frame*, which in turn is itself on the form. Moving the frame around would automatically move the other controls on that frame as well. Those controls are considered part of that frame.

To add a Frame control:

1 Double-click the Frame tool on the Toolbox to create a Frame control on the form.

2 Position the Frame tool in the upper-left corner of the form, as shown in Figure 4.3.

Again, don't worry about positioning the frame exactly; the controls will all be repositioned as necessary later.

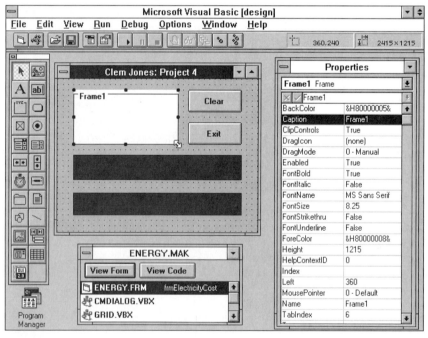

Figure 4.3

3 Type **fraSeason** as the frame's **Name** property.

4 Set the frame's **BackColor** property to solid teal, matching the form's background color.

5 Type **Season** as the **Caption** property for the frame.
The form should now resemble Figure 4.4.

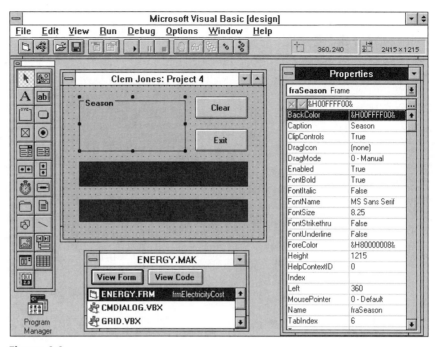

Figure 4.4

ADDING OPTION BUTTONS

Option buttons, sometimes referred to as radio buttons, exist in a group where only one of the options can be selected at a time. The options are toggled by selecting one of the option buttons. Option buttons look like small outline circles that, when selected, contain smaller filled circles. You should always include descriptive text next to each option button.

Normally, option buttons are used to choose from two or three options. If you wish for the user to have a wider range of choices, there are other controls that are better suited to the task. Typically, option buttons are displayed vertically, in a row. The top button is the *default*, or selected option, that is, the option automatically selected by the program

 ### To add option buttons to the Season frame:

 1 Double-click the Option Button control in the Toolbox to create the first button, as shown in Figure 4.5, and position the button inside the frame.

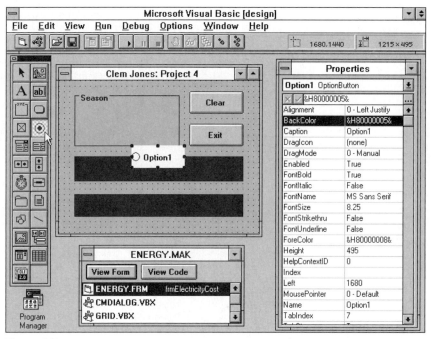

Figure 4.5

2 Create the second button in a similar manner.

3 Type **Summer** as the upper option button's **Caption** property, type **optSummer** as its Name, change its **BackColor** to match the parent form, and change its **Value** to **True**.

The Value property determines which option button is the default button. The default button will initially appear selected.

4 Type **Winter** as the lower option button's **Caption** property, type **optWinter** as its **Name**, and change its **BackColor** to match the parent form.

The form should resemble Figure 4.6.

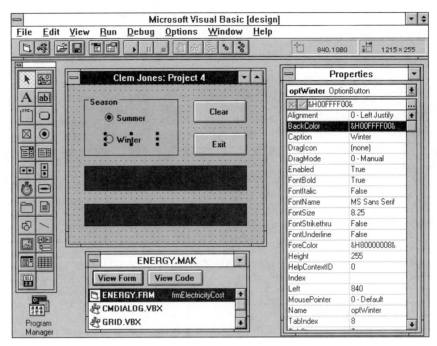

Figure 4.6

ADDING THE OTHER FRAME CONTROLS

According to the flowchart, txtKWHour and lblEstimatedCost should both be bordered by their own Frame controls. Adding pre-existing controls to a new frame is a little more complicated than creating controls after the frame already exists. Recall that the two option buttons, optSummer and optWinter, were created after fraSeason. For the next two frames, some of the controls already exist, but you haven't yet created the frames that will contain them.

To add these pre-existing controls to a new ~~form~~ *frame*, you must employ the standard cut and paste operations. Currently, txtKWHour and lblEstimatedCost reside directly on the form. If you would like to place them on a frame, you must cut them from the form and paste them onto the frame.

To add a Frame control for txtKWHour:

1 Pull the bottom border of the form down a bit to make some room, and move txtKWHour and lblEstimatedCost down to the bottom of the form.

2 Create a Frame control, and position it as shown in Figure 4.7.

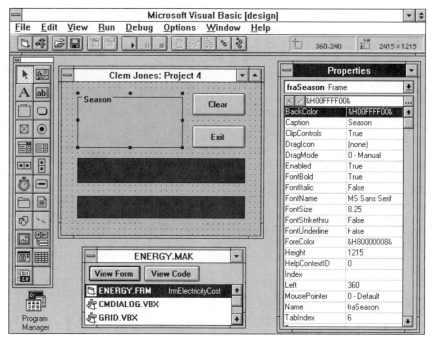

Figure 4.7

3 Type **fraKWHour** as the Frame control's **Name** property, change its **BackColor** property to match the form, and type **Kilowatt-Hours** as its **Caption** property.

The screen should now resemble Figure 4.8.

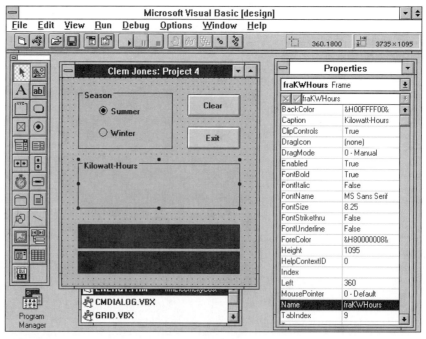

Figure 4.8

4 Resize txtKWHour so that it is small enough to fit inside of fraKWHour, as shown in Figure 4.9.

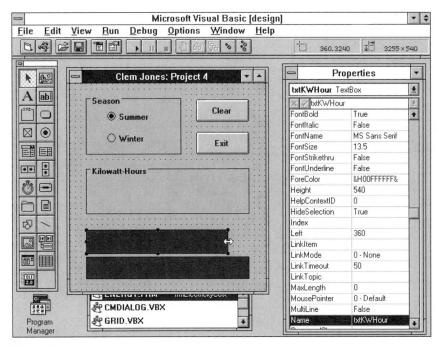

Figure 4.9

5 Make sure txtKWHour is still selected, and then choose **Edit** and **Cut**. This places txtKWHour into the clipboard.

6 Select fraKWHour, and then choose **Edit** and **Paste**. This action causes txtKWHour to be pasted onto the frame.

7 Resize and position txtKWHour so that the screen resembles Figure 4.10.

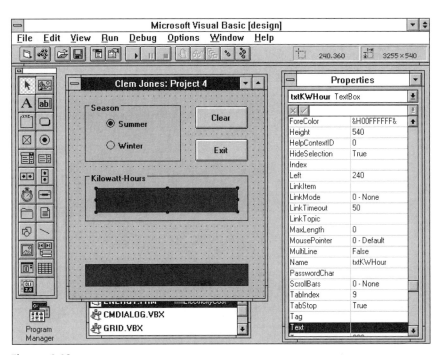

Figure 4.10

To add a frame for lblEstimatedCost:

1 Create another Frame control of the same size, and position it below fraKWHour, as shown in Figure 4.11.

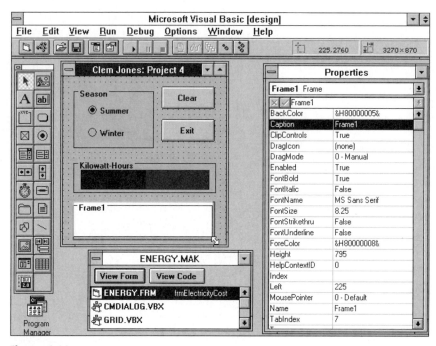

Figure 4.11

2 Type `fraEstimated` as the new frame's **Name** property, change the **BackColor** to match the form BackColor, and type `Estimated Cost` as the **Caption** property.

3 Cut and paste lblEstimated onto fraEstimated in the same manner as txtKWHour was pasted onto fraKWHour.

4 Resize lblEstimated as necessary.

5 Save your work and run the program.
Notice that the option buttons function but do not change anything—the code for the option buttons is yet to be written.

6 Stop the program.

EXIT If necessary, you can exit Visual Basic and continue this project later.

CREATING A SCROLL BAR

Anyone who has used Windows will be familiar with scroll bars. *Scroll bars*, which come in horizontal and vertical varieties, allow the user to navigate easily through a long list of information. Word processors like Microsoft Word use vertical scroll bars to allow the user to scroll, or position, the viewing window over text. Scroll bars can also be used to facilitate user input. In this project you will create a horizontal scroll bar that will be used to change the value in txtKWHour. You'll recall that Project 3 used a text box, txtKWHour, to allow user input. The scroll bar represents an alternative means to get input; that is, it provides a different way for the user to indicate how many kilowatt-hours were used.

A horizontal scroll bar consists of two *scroll arrows*, which can be selected with the mouse button to move the *scroll box* left or right. The scroll box, sometimes called the thumb, determines the current value of the scroll bar. Moving the scroll box to the right will raise the value; moving it to the left will lower the value.

To create a horizontal scroll bar:

1 Resize txtKWHour so that it only occupies the right side of fraKWHour, as shown in Figure 4.12.

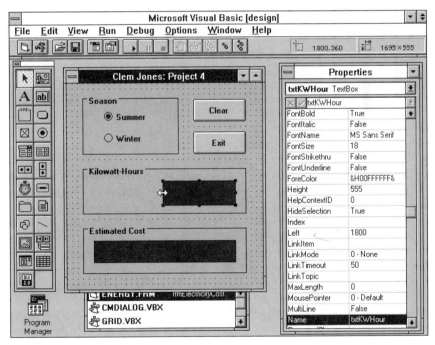

Figure 4.12

2 Select fraKWHour.
The scroll bar needs to be on the frame, not directly on the form.

3 Double-click the Horizontal Scroll Bar tool.
The screen should resemble Figure 4.13.

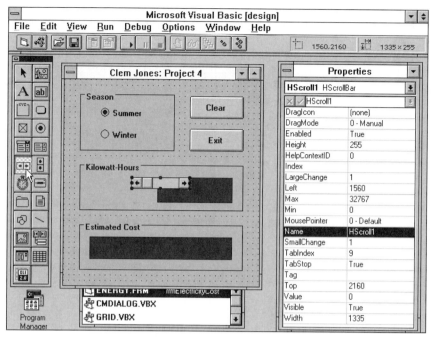

Figure 4.13

4 Position the horizontal scroll bar using Figure 4.1 as a reference guide.

At this time, you may also want to reposition any other controls on the form so that your visual design matches the flowchart.

5 Type **hsbKWHour** as the **Name** property of the horizontal scroll bar. As you can probably guess, the prefix for a horizontal scroll bar is *hsb*. The screen should now resemble Figure 4.14.

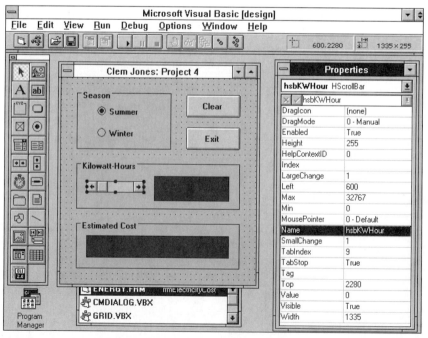

Figure 4.14

Setting Scroll Bar Properties

Scroll bar properties determine how the scroll bar behaves when clicked. Scroll bars have a range of values that are set with the Min and Max properties. Min determines the minimum value of the scroll bar. On a horizontal scroll bar, the minimum value is on the left side. For this project the minimum value should be set to zero as it wouldn't make sense for a residential electric customer to use a negative amount of kilowatt-hours. The Max value is on the right side of the scroll bar and determines the maximum value that the scroll bar will reach. If the user moves the scroll box all the way to the right, the Max value will result. You will be using a Max value of 9999.

The value that a scroll bar contains can also be changed by clicking the area between a scroll box and a scroll arrow. This causes the scroll box to move in larger increments than when the user clicks a scroll arrow. The amount that the scroll box moves in this case is set by the LargeChange property. The SmallChange property determines how far the scroll box moves (and how much the scroll bar value changes) each time the user clicks the scroll. *arrow*.

To set the scroll bar properties:

1 Type **9999** as the **Max** property for hsbKWHour.
The **Min** property is set to 0 by default and should not need to be changed.

2 Type **100** as the **LargeChange** property, and type **10** as the **SmallChange** property.

Writing Code for the Scroll Bar

You'll recall that the scroll bar you've just created is designed to facilitate user input. To accomplish this, you'll need to write code that will respond to the user's mouse clicks on the scroll bar.

Fortunately, Visual Basic handles much of the work for you. All you'll need to do is respond to one event. A change event occurs when the value of the scroll bar has changed in any way.

The Value property of the horizontal scroll bar determines the current position of the scroll box in the scroll bar. Basically, then, all you need to do is watch for the Change event by using an event procedure and then modify the Text property of txtKWHour accordingly.

To write code for the change event:

1 Double-click hsbKWHour to open its Code window.
The default procedure that appears is Change.

2 Type the following line of code at the end of the Change procedure:

```
txtKWHour.Text = Format(hsbKWHour.Value)
```

This line of code converts the numeric value of hsbKWHour.Value to a value that can be displayed as the text of txtKWHour.

3 Close the Code window and run the program.
Try clicking on the scroll bar arrows and dragging the scroll box. The scroll bar should function as planned. The option buttons, however, are not working yet.

4 Stop the program.

PROGRAMMING OPTION BUTTONS

Whenever a user of the electricity calculator selects an option button, it should cause recalculation of the electricity costs; in other words, it should call the procedure where this calculation takes place, txtKWHour_Change. The user would want recalculation to happen because winter and summer costs are computed differently. You will also want a click of an option button to set the focus back to the txtKWHour input box, to allow the user to make further changes easily.

To add code to the option buttons:

1 Select optSummer, and double-click to open its Code window.

2 Type the following lines of code to the Click event procedure, as shown in Figure 4.15:

```
txtKWHour_Change
txtKWHour.SetFocus
```

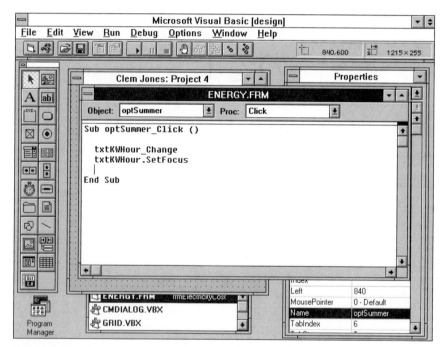

Figure 4.15

3 Add the same two lines of code to the Click event procedure of optWinter as well.

USING THE SELECT CASE STATEMENT

Sometimes your programs will need to select from among many choices. The If-Then-Else statement can be **nested**, which means that If-Then-Else statements can exist inside other If-Then-Else statements. This can quickly get confusing. Consider the following pseudocode, based on the code needed for the current project:

```
If KWHours > 0 And KWHours < 400 Then
    compute cost here
Else
  If KWHours < 800 Then
    compute cost here
  Else
    compute cost here
  EndIf
EndIf
```

As you can see, this is a little convoluted. Fortunately, Visual Basic offers the **Select Case statement**, which can replace multiple nested If-Then-Else statements, making your program easier to code, read, and understand.

The Select Case statement differs from If-Then-Else in that it tests whether an expression falls within a range of values; If-Then-Else only determines if an expression is true or false. The Select Case statement takes the following form:

```
Select Case expression
  Case test
    instruction block
  Case test
    instruction block
  Case Else
    instruction block
End Select
```

where *expression* can be any standard Visual Basic expression, *test* is one or more test ranges, and *instruction block* is a block of one or more Visual Basic instructions. This example includes two test cases, but remember that there can be any number of test cases.

The range of values that the Select Case statement can test is far more powerful than the true or false test that If-Then-Else performs. The following table lists the range types and an example of each.

Range Type	Example
Equality	Case Is = 50
	Case 50
Explicit Range	Case 10 to 20
Multiple	Case Is > 10, Is < 20
Relational	Case Is <= 20

A Select Case statement, then, can look something like the following example. Obviously, this example is not the most efficient code. It is provided only to show the use of various range types.

```
Select Case SchoolYear
  Case 1
    YearName = "freshman"
  Case Is > 1, Is < 3
    YearName = "sophomore"
  Case Is = 3
    YearName = "junior"
  Case 4
    YearName = "senior"
  Else
    YearName = "not enrolled in school"
End Select
```

CHANGING THE WAY COST IS COMPUTED

You will have to make a decision based on which option button, Summer or Winter, is selected. The cost computation for winter electricity usage is going to change dramatically. To accommodate the various winter electricity rates, you will need to add a few new constants to the txtKWHour_Change procedure. A Select Case statement will be used to determine the cost if the winter option is selected.

The following code is a mixture of pseudocode and actual source code that uses the Select Case statement and takes into account the new sliding scale for winter electricity costs.

> *Reminder* When typing Visual Basic code, use the same spacing and indenting style as the code examples presented in this module.

```
If the Summer option button is "True" (selected) Then
  Cost is kilowatt-hours used times the summer cost per kilowatt-hour
Else
  Select Case kilowatt-hours
    Case 0 to 400
      Cost = WinterBasicFee + kilowatt-hours * WinterCost1st400
    Case 401 to 800
      Cost = WinterBasicFee + 400 * WinterCost1st400
      Cost = Cost + (kilowatt-hours - 400) * WinterCost2nd400
    Case Is >= 801
      Cost = WinterBasicFee + 400 * WinterCost1st400
      Cost = Cost + 400 * WinterCost2nd400
      Cost = Cost + (kilowatt-hours - 800) * WinterCostOver800
  End Select
End If
```

Cost is calculated using a sliding scale in conformance with the specifications.

Notice that the Select Case statement is the Else part of the original If statement. The Select Case should only occur if the user chooses the Winter option button. There is nothing wrong with using the Select Case statement this way. In fact, you could conceivably have combinations of Select Case statements nested inside If-Then-Else statements or vice versa. How you tackle a particular programming assignment is up to you, but remember to choose decision constructs that are easy to read and understand.

To modify the code:

1 Select txtKWHour, and double-click to open its Code window.

2 Modify the constant declarations (constants are defined with the Const keyword) in the click event procedure, as shown in Figure 4.16.

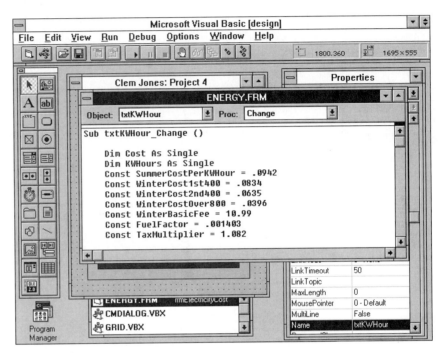

Figure 4.16

3 Change the ~~Click~~ *Change* Event procedure by typing the following code:

```
Dim Cost As Single
Dim KWHours As Single
Const SummerCostPerKWHour = .0942
Const WinterCost1st400 = .0834
Const WinterCost2nd400 = .0635
Const WinterCostOver800 = .0396
Const WinterBasicFee = 10.99
Const FuelFactor = .001403
Const TaxMultiplier = 1.082

KWHours = Val(txtKWHour.Text)

If optSummer.Value = True Then
  Cost = KWHours * SummerCostPerKWHour
Else
  Select Case KWHours
    Case 0 To 400
      Cost = WinterBasicFee + KWHours * WinterCost1st400
    Case 401 To 800
      Cost = WinterBasicFee + 400 * WinterCost1st400
      Cost = Cost + (KWHours - 400) * WinterCost2nd400
    Case Else
      Cost = WinterBasicFee + 400 * WinterCost1st400
```

```
        Cost = Cost + 400 * WinterCost2nd400
        Cost = Cost + (KWHours - 800) * WinterCostOver800
    End Select
End If

Cost = Cost - KWHours * FuelFactor
Cost = Cost * TaxMultiplier
lblEstimatedCost.Caption = Format(Cost, "$ ##,##0.00")
```

4 Close the Code window, and save the project.

5 Run and test the program.

Notice that selecting the option buttons now affects the estimated cost.

6 Stop the program.

VALIDATING INPUT

Only a few more refinements need to be made to the program. Currently, changing the value of txtKWHour by typing numbers in the text box does not move the scroll button on the scroll bar, but it should. Also, it is possible for the user to enter values that are out of range. Remember that the Min and Max properties for hsbKWHour are set to 0 and 9999, respectively. If a user enters a value less than 0 or more than 9999, an error will result. This type of error checking is easy to perform in Visual Basic.

To add input validation code:

1 Open the txtKWHour_Change procedure by double-clicking txtKWHour.

2 Type the following lines using Figure 4.17 as a model.

```
If KWHours > 9999 Then KWHours = 9999
If KWHours < 0 Then KWHours = 0
txtKWHour.Text = KWHours
hsbKWHour.Value = Int(KWHours)
```

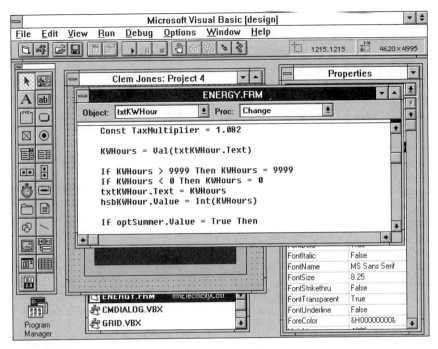

Figure 4.17

3 Close the Code window.

4 Run and test the program.

5 Stop the program, and save your work.

THE NEXT STEP

This concludes your investigation into electricity cost calculation. Project 4 built upon the base that was begun in Project 3, adding seasonal cost adjustments and some new controls: the frame, option buttons, and a horizontal scroll bar. Use of these controls offers the programmer a logical way to present options, and allows the user to interact with your programs in an obvious and friendly way. You have also been exposed to some more complex branching techniques, the nested If-Then-Else statement and its more elegant replacement, the Select Case statement. These powerful constructs will enable your program to quickly and easily respond to the need of the user.

The next project will be a little more entertaining. You will create a computerized slot machine complete with spinning reels. This project will include some simple animated reels and a scoring system.

This concludes Project 4. You can either exit Visual Basic, or go on to work the Study Questions, Review Exercises, and Assignments.

SUMMARY AND EXERCISES

Summary

- Option buttons, arranged in a group, are used for mutually exclusive choices.
- Option buttons are usually arranged vertically, and the top button is the default, or automatically selected, button.
- The standard event associated with option buttons is the mouse Click event.
- The Select Case statement can efficiently replace nested If-Then-Else statements.
- The Select Case statement tests whether an expression falls within a range of values.
- Frame controls are used to visually arrange other controls into logical groups.
- Horizontal scroll bars provide an easy way for the user to enter input, change data, or navigate through a list of information.

Key Terms and Operations

Key Terms	**Operations**
default	Add a frame to an existing program
Frame control	Base calculations on a sliding scale
nested	Create a horizontal scroll bar
option button	Create option buttons
scroll arrow	Group controls within a frame
scroll bar	Set option button properties
scroll box	Use option buttons
Select Case statement	Use the Select Case statement to replace nested If-Then-Else statements
	Write code for option buttons
	Write code for scroll bar events

Study Questions

Multiple Choice

1. How many option buttons in a group can be selected at once?
   a. all
   b. two
   c. three
   d. one
   e. none

2. The default option button in a group is
   a. the middle one.
   b. the top one.
   c. the one on the far left.
   d. the bottom one.
   e. none—it is chosen by the programmer.

3. What are Frame controls used for?
   a. to group frames
   b. to group Form windows
   c. to connect text with a line
   d. to group option buttons (controls)
   e. to hold images

4. What is the naming prefix for an option button?
   a. option
   b. optn
   c. opt
   d. Option
   e. Opt

5. The Select Case statement
   a. allows decision branching.
   b. makes choices for the user.
   c. prompts the user to make a choice.
   d. is designed to replace the GOTO statement.
   e. requires complicated nesting.

6. Select Case is a good replacement for what statements?
   a. nested robins
   b. nested For-Do-Thens
   c. convoluted Ifs
   d. lateral If-Then-Elses
   e. nested If-Then-Elses

7. The Select Case statement tests whether an expression
   a. falls within a range of values.
   b. is true or false only.
   c. evaluates to a non-zero value.
   d. is grammatically correct.
   e. can be selected.

8. The two types of scroll bars are
   a. horizontal and equal.
   b. true and false.
   c. verifiable and vertical.
   d. frames and forms.
   e. horizontal and vertical.

9. The range of values a scroll bar can have are determined by
   a. the Min and Max properties.
   b. Windows.
   c. the user.
   d. the Minimum and Maximum values in the Range property.
   e. the Minimum and Maximum properties.

10. Which property determines the current position of the scroll box in
    the scroll bar?
    a. Current
    b. Value
    c. Place
    d. IsHere
    e. Box

Short Answer

1. Can two option buttons in the same group be selected simultaneously?

2. What shape is an option button?

3. Is the Frame control something that the user would click on normally?

4. Why would a Frame control be helpful on a form with two or more option button groups?

5. How is Select Case different from If-Then-Else?

6. Why is Select Case preferable to several nested If-Then-Else statements?

7. What are the various uses for a scroll bar?

8. What event would be caused by the user clicking a scroll bar arrow?

9. How do you set the minimum and maximum values that a scroll bar is capable of supporting?

10. What is the prefix for a horizontal scroll bar?

For Discussion

1. The Select Case statement is far more versatile than the If-Then-Else. Discuss times when either looping contract would be more appropriate.

2. How are Frame controls used in the Windows environment?

3. Option buttons are usually used when the user is presented with two or three choices. Why would it be inappropriate to use option buttons when there are ten choices to be made?

4. A scroll bar can be used to facilitate user input with the mouse instead of the keyboard. Is this always appropriate?

Review Exercises

Creating an Astro Scale

The weight of an object on the surface of a planet depends on the gravitational attraction between the object and the planet, which in turn depends on the mass and radius of each. Your weight on another planet might be more or less than your weight on the Earth. If you know your weight on Earth, you can calculate your weight on another planet by multiplying your Earth weight by a conversion factor appropriate for the other planet.

For example, the moon's factor is 0.16; this means that your weight on the moon is only 16 percent of your weight on the Earth. If you weigh 100 pounds on Earth, you would only weigh 16 pounds on the moon.

Construct an application similar to Figure 4.18. Users should be able to enter their weights on earth and choose an option button to find out what their weights would be on any of the following celestial bodies: the moon, Mars, Jupiter, and Pluto. Though Jupiter is a gas giant with no distinct surface, its gravitational factor is included here for fun. Here are the relative weight factors (Earth = 1.0):

Moon   0.16

Mars   0.39

Jupiter   2.54

Pluto   0.06

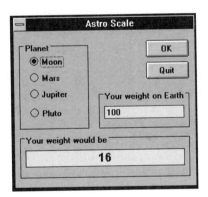

Figure 4.18

Creating a Postal Calculator

Create an express mail cost calculator similar to Figure 4.19.

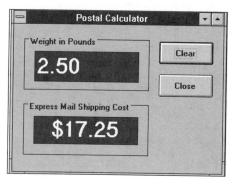

Figure 4.19

The cost of sending a package should be calculated according to the following method:

Total Cost	Weight Range (in Pounds)
$10.75	Weight > 0 and weight <= 0.5
$15.00	Weight > 0.5 and weight <= 2.0
$17.25	Weight > 2.0 and weight <= 3.0
$19.40	Weight > 3.0 and weight <= 4.0
$21.55	Weight > 4.0 and weight <= 5.0

Weights above 5 pounds should not be accepted by the calculator.

Assignments

Improving the Astro Scale

Using the first review exercise in this project as a guide, improve the astro scale to include a horizontal scroll bar that will allow you to scroll through a range of weights, from 0 to 300 pounds, that can be converted to relative weights on other planets. The scroll bar and a Label control (used to display the value of the scroll bar) will replace the text box used in the first review exercise. Your program should resemble Figure 4.20 when it is completed.

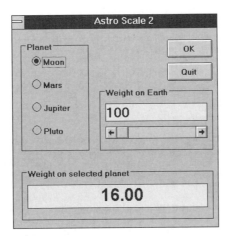

Figure 4.20

Creating an Astro Postal Calculator

This exercise combines the two review exercises. Create an astro postal calculator that will take the weight of a package in earth pounds and convert it to its appropriate weight on another planet based on which option button is selected. Then, using the cost chart from the second review exercise in this project, the program will calculate the cost for shipping that package on the appropriate planet. Your program should resemble Figure 4.21.

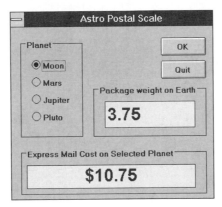

Figure 4.21

Creating a Loan Calculator

The Visual Basic Pmt function can be used to calculate the periodic payment on a loan. The variables used in an ordinary loan are the principle (the amount borrowed), the term or number of periods (the number of payments made), and the periodic interest rate. The periodic interest rate and the term must be expressed in the same time units (for example, months).

Suppose you borrow $5000 at 15 percent annual interest for a term of five years. Since payments are made monthly on most loans, the periodic interest rate is 15% / 12, and the term is 5 * 12. Visual Basic can be used to calculate the monthly payment following this general formula:

```
Monthly Payment = -Pmt(Periodic Interest Rate,
        No. Periods, Principle,0,0)
```

Since Pmt returns a negative number to represent cash outflow, a minus sign is used in the above formula to reverse the sign. The two zeros are arguments that you must include but are not relevant for this assignment.

Build a loan calculator as shown in Figure 4.22 that allows the user to specify principle, annual interest, and term in years. The program should calculate monthly payment any time a change is made to the text boxes for the principal, periodic interest rate, or term.

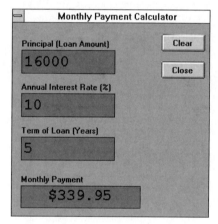

Figure 4.22

PROJECT 5: CREATING A COMPUTER SLOT MACHINE

Objectives

After completing this project, you should be able to:

▶ Use Image controls to display pictures

▶ Use Shape controls to display borders

▶ Use the Timer control to cause periodic execution of code

▶ Specify a variable's lifetime by using the Dim and Static statements

▶ Generate random numbers using the Rnd function and the Randomize statement

CASE STUDY: CREATING A SLOT MACHINE PROGRAM

Computers are not only used to run business spreadsheets and accounting software. In fact, one of the fastest growing areas of computer software sales is in entertainment. Games and multimedia programs dominate the software best-seller charts, a testament to their popularity. In this project and the next, you will design and create a computer slot machine. It will feature graphics and even some simple animation. Granted, Nintendo has nothing to fear: The program you will create is a first tentative step into the waters of entertainment software design. It will, however, offer a glimpse into the powerful yet easy way that Visual Basic can manipulate graphic images.

Designing the Solution

This program will use bitmapped graphics to display the items on a slot machine reel. These images will be changed over a period of time to simulate the spinning of the reels. As each reel stops spinning, a border shape will appear around each reel.

The program you will develop here will provide the basis for Project 6, in which you will improve the slot machine's performance and make it easier to use.

The specifications for this program are as follows:

- The user should be presented with a window, as illustrated in the flow-charts shown in Figures 5.1 and 5.2. The window will consist of three reels, a Spin button, a current score indicator, a session total score indicator, and a Close button.

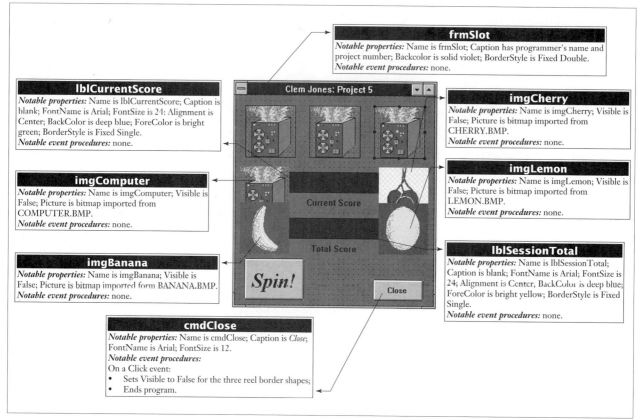

frmSlot
Notable properties: Name is frmSlot; Caption has programmer's name and project number; Backcolor is solid violet; BorderStyle is Fixed Double.
Notable event procedures: none.

lblCurrentScore
Notable properties: Name is lblCurrentScore; Caption is blank; FontName is Arial; FontSize is 24; Alignment is Center; BackColor is deep blue; ForeColor is bright green; BorderStyle is Fixed Single.
Notable event procedures: none.

imgComputer
Notable properties: Name is imgComputer; Visible is False; Picture is bitmap imported from COMPUTER.BMP.
Notable event procedures: none.

imgBanana
Notable properties: Name is imgBanana; Visible is False; Picture is bitmap imported form BANANA.BMP.
Notable event procedures: none.

cmdClose
Notable properties: Name is cmdClose; Caption is *Close*; FontName is Arial; FontSize is 12.
Notable event procedures:
On a Click event:
- Sets Visible to False for the three reel border shapes;
- Ends program.

imgCherry
Notable properties: Name is imgCherry; Visible is False; Picture is bitmap imported from CHERRY.BMP.
Notable event procedures: none.

imgLemon
Notable properties: Name is imgLemon; Visible is False; Picture is bitmap imported from LEMON.BMP.
Notable event procedures: none.

lblSessionTotal
Notable properties: Name is lblSessionTotal; Caption is blank; FontName is Arial; FontSize is 24; Alignment is Center, BackColor is deep blue; ForeColor is bright yellow; BorderStyle is Fixed Single.
Notable event procedures: none.

Figure 5.1

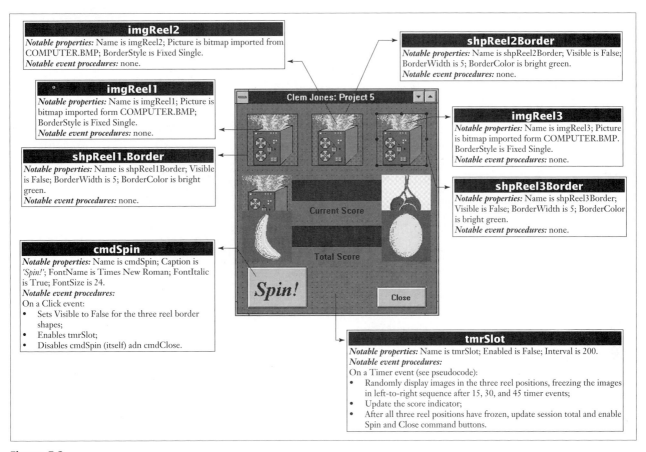

Figure 5.2

- The three reels should initially display images of a sparking mainframe computer when the program is first run.
- When the user clicks the Spin button, each reel should show an image randomly selected from the following list:

Image	Bitmap File	Point Value
Computer	COMPUTER.BMP	0
Lemon	LEMON.BMP	1
Banana	BANANA.BMP	2
Cherry	CHERRY.BMP	3

- New images for each reel should be selected randomly by the program and displayed after a brief time interval.
- A moment-to-moment point value should appear in the current score indicator as the images change. This is computed by summing the point values for the image currently displayed in each reel and then multiplying the result by 100.
- The Spin and Close buttons should be disabled while the reels are spinning.
- Eventually, the images in each reel should freeze, starting with the left reel after a short time, then the middle reel, and finally the right reel.
- As each image freezes, a bright green border should appear around the reel.

- When all three have frozen, the session total score indicator should be incremented by the final value of the current score indicator, and the Spin and Close buttons should once again be enabled.
- When the user clicks the Close button, the program should stop.

Using the OPE Flowcharts

Figures 5.1 and 5.2 show flowcharts for this project (two flowcharts are used because of the large number of controls on the form). You will make extensive use of these flowcharts when building the program. Now that you are more experienced with Visual Basic, the steps presented for completion of this project will be somewhat abbreviated.

To build the form and define the basic controls:

1 Open and save a new form as SLOT.FRM and a new project as SLOT.MAK.

2 Create the following objects and assign only their properties. Refer to the flowcharts in Figures 5.1 and 5.2.

Object	Function
frmSlot	The form
lblCurrentScore	Displays the current score
lblSessionTotal	Displays the total score for the current session
lblCurrentDescription	Heading for current score
lblSessionDescription	Heading for total score
cmdSpin	Spin command button
cmdClose	Command button to end the program

The screen should look similiar to Figure 5.3.

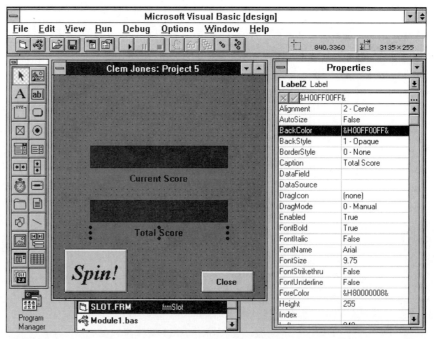

Figure 5.3

Unfortunately, the form itself will be too large to manage easily on the screen in regular VGA resolution. You may have to get used to overlapping windows.

> **Reminder** You can click a partly obscured window's title bar (or other area of the window) to bring it to the foreground.

You will probably have to resize the form and controls as you add to your program. Don't worry if it isn't perfect right away. The important thing now is to get the basic controls on the form. Assign the properties to the form and controls listed above, but do not write any event procedure code yet.

CREATING IMAGE CONTROLS

An *Image control* is used to display a picture. The Picture property is used to assign a filename to each image control. The filename should contain the full path of the image you would like to display: that is, it should specify not only the image's filename but also its disk and directory location. For example, if the image file you are using is called KANGAROO.BMP and it resides in the C:\WINDOWS directory, you would set the Picture property for that image control to C:\WINDOWS\KANGAROO.BMP.

The four images used in this program have been supplied to your instructor and should be copied to the floppy disk you have been using. The filenames are BANANA.BMP, CHERRY.BMP, LEMON.BMP, and COMPUTER.BMP. The BMP extension stands for *bitmapped graphic*.

> **Tip** If you like, you can create your own image files using the Paintbrush accessory that comes with Windows. Once in Paintbrush, you will need to choose Image Attributes from the Options menu and specify a color image of 80 x 80 pels, or pixels. Remember to save each picture before designing another one.

For the slot machine program to display each of the four images easily, you must create a separate Image control for each picture. This makes the images available for later use in the reels at the top of the window. In the steps that follow, you will import the four bitmaps, assigning each to a separate Image control. The Visible property on each control will be set to False: You will not want the four images to display when the program starts, but they will need to be on the form so that they are available for later use.

To create the the first Image control:

1 Select an Image control by double-clicking the Image Control icon in the Toolbox.
As shown in Figure 5.4, an Image control appears in the center of the form.

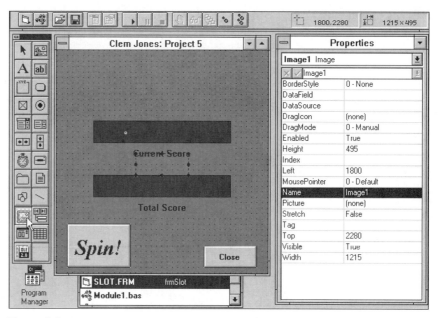

Figure 5.4

2 Drag the Image control to the left side of the form.
Don't worry about the control's size; it will automatically resize to fit the image that will be imported.

3 Activate the Properties window, and double-click on the **Picture** property.
As shown in Figure 5.5, a Load Picture dialog box appears that allows you to choose an image file and assign it to the Image control.

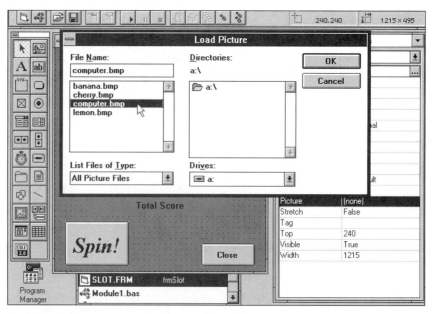

Figure 5.5

4 Change to drive A (or to the drive and directory that contains the bitmap image files), and double-click COMPUTER.BMP
The image of the computer fills the Image control, as shown in Figure 5.6.

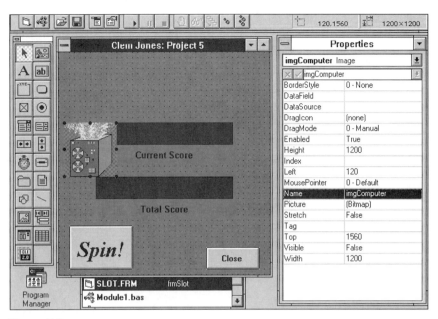

Figure 5.6

The size of the Image control is automatically adjusted to fit the picture.

5 Type **imgComputer** as the **Name** property of the Image control.
As you've no doubt guessed, the prefix for an Image control Name is *img*.

6 Change the **Visible** property to **False**.
This ensures that the image will not initially display when the program
runs. Because the image will not be visible when the program is running,
it is not very important where you place it on the form.

7 Run the program to confirm that the Image control does not display,
as shown in Figure 5.7.

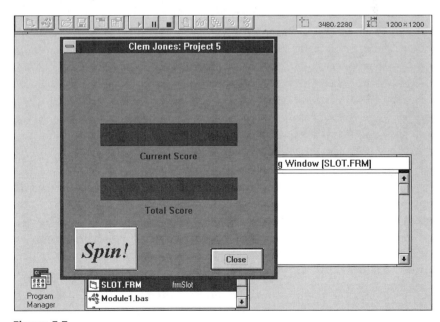

Figure 5.7

8 Stop the program.

To create the remaining Image controls:

1 Referring to Figure 5.1 and following procedures similar to the steps you just completed, create these Image controls:

imgBanana   BANANA.BMP
imgLemon   LEMON.BMP
imgCherry   CHERRY.BMP

Remember to assign the appropriate **Name** property and to set the **Visible** property to **False** for each image. The images can be placed anywhere on the form. The screen should resemble Figure 5.8.

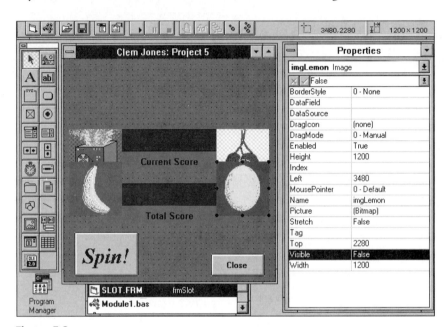

Figure 5.8

2 Run the program to ensure that none of the images appear.

3 Stop the program.

4 Save your work.

ADDING IMAGES

The three reels at the top of the window will initially display the computer image, but they will also display the other images in a randomly changing sequence.

To add the three reel images:

1 Create three Image controls named imgReel1, imgReel2, and imgReel3, and place them in a row at the top of the form.
The screen should resemble Figure 5.2.

2 Assign the **Picture** property of each reel to the COMPUTER.BMP bitmap.

3 Set the **BorderStyle** property of each reel to **1 - Fixed Single**.

4 If necessary, move the controls around on the form so that they more closely resemble Figure 5.9.

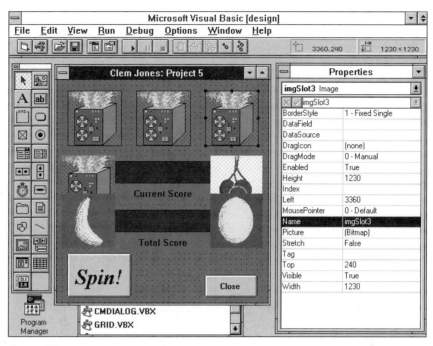

Figure 5.9

ADDING SHAPES

The *Shape control* allows you to display simple graphical objects like rectangles, ovals, or rounded rectangles directly on a form. These shapes are used primarily in backgrounds because they are not very detailed. They are also nice for providing visual feedback. You will use a rectangular shape to show that the slot machine has finished spinning through the sets of images. The rectangular shape you will create will form a border around each reel image.

The specifications call for a bright green bordering shape to appear on a reel once it stops changing and stays on a particular final image. In the steps that follow, you will create the border shapes. They will initially have their Visible properties set to False; when a reel stops, the shape that surrounds it will have its Visible property set to True. As you complete these steps, refer once again to the flowchart shown in Figure 5.2.

To add the bordering shapes:

1 Click the Shape tool in the Toolbox.
The default shape is a rectangle.

2 Drag the crosshairs around imgReel1 to form a well-spaced border around the reel image, as shown in Figure 5.10.

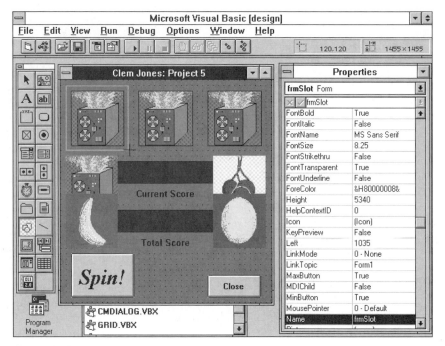

Figure 5.10

3 Type **shpReel1Border** as the **Name** property of the shape.
The prefix for a Shape name is *shp*.

4 Change the **Visible** property to **False**.

5 Change the **BorderWidth** property to **5**.

6 Change the **BorderColor** property to bright green.

7 In a similar manner, create shpReel2Border and shpReel3Border, setting their properties as documented in Figure 5.2.
The screen should now resemble Figure 5.11.

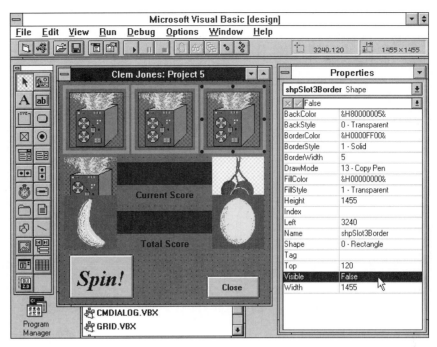

Figure 5.11

ADDING A TIMER CONTROL

A **Timer control** acts independently of the user, responding to the passage of time. It is an unusual control because it is not a visual resource: It never appears in the window of a running program. Timers cause events to occur at specific time intervals. Once a timer is enabled, it sends **timer event messages** at whatever time intervals you set it for. Whenever a timer event occurs, the corresponding **Timer Event procedure** executes. You write the code for the Timer Event procedure.

A Timer control uses the Interval property to specify the number of milliseconds (1 millisecond = 1/1000 or 0.001 second) that pass between one timer event and the next. The interval must be between 0 and 64,767, inclusive. Since 64,767 milliseconds translates to roughly 65 seconds, every thousand milliseconds is one second in "real time." The Interval property is not very accurate, however, and should not be used for anything critical.

To add a Timer control to the slot machine program:

1 Double-click on the Timer tool in the Toolbox to place a Timer control in the center of the form.
The screen should resemble Figure 5.12.

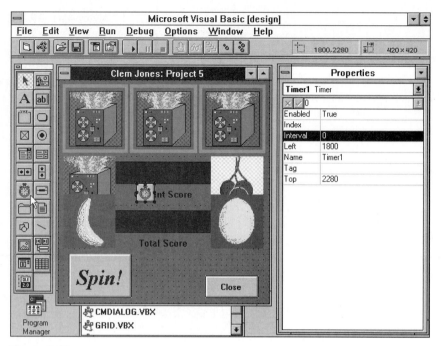

Figure 5.12

2 Place the Timer control anywhere on the form.
Because the Timer control isn't going to be visible to the user, it really doesn't matter where you place it.

3 Type **tmrSlot** as the **Name** property.

4 Set the **Interval** property to **200**.
This Interval setting will cause a timer event roughly five times a second.

5 Change the **Enabled** property to **False**.
The screen should now resemble Figure 5.13.

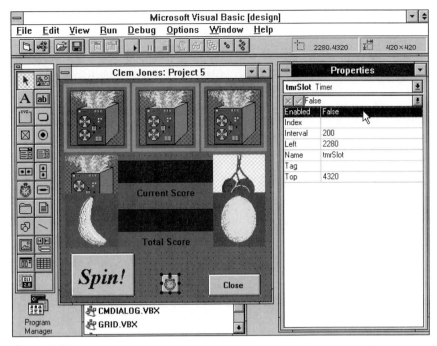

Figure 5.13

6 Save your work.

EXIT If necessary, you can exit Visual Basic now and continue this project later.

DETERMINING THE LIFETIME OF A VARIABLE

Each variable you create in Visual Basic has a *lifetime*, which defines when the variable is created at runtime. When a variable is declared in a procedure with the Dim statement, that variable exists in memory *only when that particular procedure is running*. When the procedure ends, that variable is gone, erased from memory.

So what happens if you declare a variable with Dim, execute the procedure, exit the procedure, and then rerun the same procedure? Because the variable ceases to exist when the procedure ends, rerunning the procedure recreates and reinitializes it, setting it to zero.

> **Reminder** The lifetime of a variable declared with Dim is the lifetime of the procedure in which it is declared. The variable exists in memory only when code in that procedure is running.

You can force Visual Basic to preserve the value of a variable by declaring it using the **Static statement** instead of Dim. Variables declared using the Static keyword do not get re-initialized every time the procedure they are part of gets executed. The lifetime of a Static variable is the life of the *program*. It can be said that these variables persist; that is, they keep their values even after the procedure they are declared in has ended.

You declare variables with Static in the same way that you use Dim:

```
Dim Total1
Static Total2
```

In this declaration, Total1 would be destroyed, or erased, every time the procedure in which it is declared is finished. Total2, however, would remain in memory for the life of the program.

> **Reminder** The lifetime of a Static variable is the lifetime of the entire program.

EXPERIMENTING WITH THE TIMER

The code you write in the Timer Event procedure of tmrSlot will execute whenever a timer event is generated (once every 200 milliseconds, in this case). To understand better how this works, you will create an Integer variable called Counter within tmrSlot_Timer. Each time tmrSlot_Timer is called, the current value of Counter will be displayed using lblCurrentScore, and Counter will be incremented.

You will use the Static statement to declare Counter, because the value of Counter should be preserved each time the procedure is executed.

To add code to the tmrSlot_Click procedure:

1 Select tmrSlot, and double-click to open its Code window.

2 Enter the following code within the procedure:

```
Static Counter As Integer
lblCurrentScore.Caption = Counter
Counter = Counter + 1
```

3 Close the Code window.

4 Run the program.

As shown in Figure 5.14, nothing happens because the timer has not been enabled.

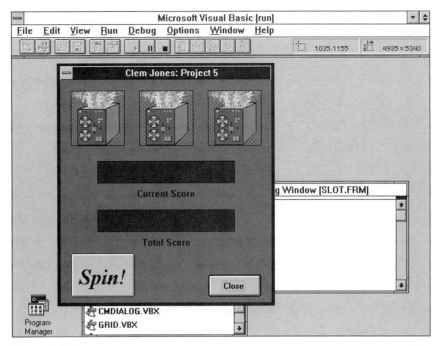

Figure 5.14

 5 Stop the program.

To enable the Timer control:

1 Modify the cmdSpin_Click procedure so that it contains the following code:

```
tmrSlot.Enabled = True
```

This will cause tmrSlot to be enabled when the user clicks on the Spin command button. The Spin button should also disable itself and the Close button while the reels are spinning.

2 Add the following lines of code to the cmdSpin_Click procedure:

```
cmdSpin.Enabled = False
cmdClose.Enabled = False
```

3 Close the Code window.

4 Open the Code window for cmdClose and add an **End** statement to the click event procedure.

5 Close the Code window.

6 Run the program, as shown in Figure 5.15, and select the Spin button. The value of Counter displays in the current score label, and the display changes each time the timer "ticks."

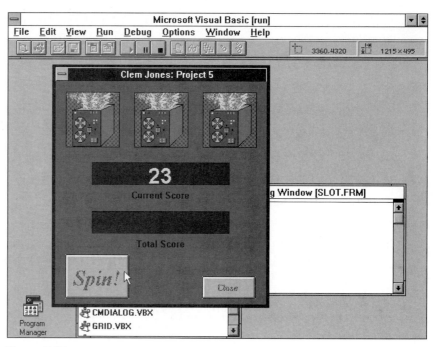

Figure 5.15

 7 Stop the program: You'll have to use the toolbar or your program's Control-menu box, since you have not yet written code to enable the Close button.

CREATING RANDOM NUMBERS

The program that you are developing needs to create random numbers so that it can simulate the spinning reels of a slot machine. Your program will use randomly generated numbers to decide which image it will display in each reel. Random numbers can be chosen using the **Rnd function**. Rnd produces a random number between 0 and 1 (for example, 0.545779). Your program needs to generate four integers between 0 and 3 (0,1,2, and 3), corresponding to the four images.

To use the function to generate random integers between 0 and 3, you will use the following expression:

```
Int(Rnd*4)
```

which extracts the integer part of the product of Rnd*4.

A **Randomize statement** will also need to be placed near the top of the code. Randomize initializes the random number generator in Visual Basic. If the Randomize statement is not executed, Rnd will generate the same sequence of "random" numbers every time you run the program. Traditional computerized random number generators actually create "pseudo-random" numbers. As John Von Neumann, a pioneer in the conceptualization of how computers should be designed, pointed out: "Anyone who considers arithmetical methods of producing random digits is, of course, in a state of sin."

Using the Timer to Change a Reel Image

The purpose of the timer in this program will be to spin the reels—to cause them to change randomly from one image to another. You will begin by experimenting with the first reel.

You will create three integer variables, Reel1Stop, Reel2Stop, and Reel3Stop, which will hold the randomly chosen image code values for each reel. Initially, you will experiment with just Reel1Stop. The Picture property of Reel1Image will be changed based on the value of Reel1Stop.

Finally, to prepare for calculation and display of numerical scores, you will create integer variables for CurrentScore and SessionTotalScore.

To change a reel image using the timer:

1 Double-click tmrSlot to open its Code window.

2 Modify the code so that it appears as follows. Note that the line that displayed the value of Counter has been removed.

```
Static Counter As Integer
Static Reel1Stop, Reel2Stop, Reel3Stop As Integer
Static CurrentScore, SessionTotalScore As Integer

Randomize
Reel1Stop = Int(Rnd * 4)
Select Case Reel1Stop
  Case 0
    imgReel1.Picture = imgComputer.Picture
  Case 1
    imgReel1.Picture = imgLemon.Picture
  Case 2
    imgReel1.Picture = imgBanana.Picture
  Case 3
    imgReel1.Picture = imgCherry.Picture
End Select

Counter = Counter + 1
```

3 Close the Code window, run the program, and then click the Spin button.

The imgReel1 picture should change randomly among the four images available. If a particular image occasionally seems to persist much longer than the others, it was probably selected and displayed two or more times in succession by chance, as shown in Figure 5.16.

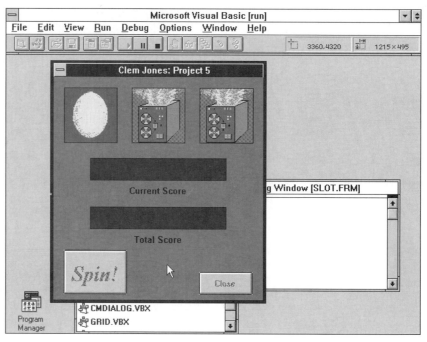

Figure 5.16

4 Stop the program using the Control-menu box or the Stop button on the toolbar in the Visual Basic Main window.

CONTROLLING WHEN THE REELS STOP

The reel images are not supposed to change indefinitely. According to the specifications, imgReel1 should stop after 15 timer ticks, imgReel2 after 30, and imgReel3 after 45. You will use the Counter variable with an If statement to determine when to stop each reel. Once a reel stops, the border shape should appear around the final image.

To control when imgReel1 stops cycling:

1 Open the Code window for tmrSlot, and modify the code for Reel1 in the tmrSlot_Timer procedure so it appears as shown in the following code.

Observe that some of the code here was presented previously. It is not necessary to erase all of the code and start over: Use your editing skills to fill in only the code that is not already in this procedure.

```
Static Counter As Integer
Static Reel1Stop, Reel2Stop, Reel3Stop As Integer
Static CurrentScore, SessionTotalScore As Integer

If Counter < 15 Then
  Randomize
  Reel1Stop = Int(Rnd * 4)
  Select Case Reel1Stop
    Case 0
      imgReel1.Picture = imgComputer.Picture
    Case 1
      imgReel1.Picture = imgLemon.Picture
    Case 2
      imgReel1.Picture = imgBanana.Picture
  Case 3
      imgReel1.Picture = imgCherry.Picture
  End Select
Else
  shpReel1Border.Visible = True
End If

Counter = Counter + 1
```

2 Close the Code window, and run and test the program.
After changing the image 15 times, Reel1 should stop and its border
shape should appear as shown in Figure 5.17.

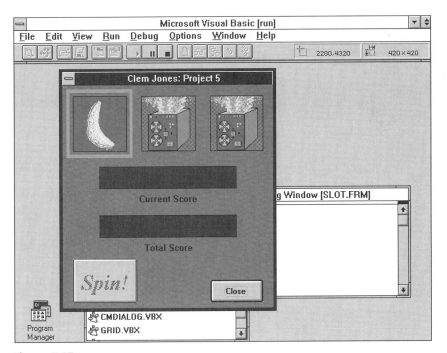

Figure 5.17

3 Stop the program, and save your work.
Now that you have gotten the first reel to cycle through a group of
images, it is time to make the other two reels follow suit.

To control when imgReel2 and imgReel3 cycle and stop:

1 Using the menu commands **Copy** and **Paste** commands on the **Edit** menu, copy the large If statement so that three such statements appear in sequence in tmrSlot_Timer. The following shows what the code should look like:

```
Static Counter As Integer
Static Reel1Stop, Reel2Stop, Reel3Stop As Integer
Static CurrentScore, SessionTotalScore As Integer

Randomize

If Counter < 15 Then
  Reel1Stop = Int(Rnd * 4)
  Select Case Reel1Stop
    Case 0
      imgReel1.Picture = imgComputer.Picture
    Case 1
      imgReel1.Picture = imgLemon.Picture
    Case 2
      imgReel1.Picture = imgBanana.Picture
    Case 3
      imgReel1.Picture = imgCherry.Picture
  End Select
Else
  shpReel1Border.Visible = True
End If
If Counter < 30 Then
Reel2Stop = Int(Rnd * 4)
Select Case Reel2Stop
  Case 0
    imgReel2.Picture = imgComputer.Picture
  Case 1
    imgReel2.Picture = imgLemon.Picture
  Case 2
    imgReel2.Picture = imgBanana.Picture
  Case 3
    imgReel2.Picture = imgCherry.Picture
  End Select
Else
    shpReel2Border.Visible = True
End If
If Counter < 45 Then
  Reel3Stop = Int(Rnd * 4)
  Select Case Reel3Stop
    Case 0
      imgReel3.Picture = imgComputer.Picture
    Case 1
      imgReel3.Picture = imgLemon.Picture
    Case 2
      imgReel3.Picture = imgBanana.Picture
    Case 3
      imgReel3.Picture = imgCherry.Picture
  End Select
```

```
Else
  shpReel3Border.Visible = True
End If

Counter = Counter + 1
```

Note that the modifications involve many small editing changes (for example, Reel1Stop becomes Reel2Stop or Reel3Stop). Be careful!

> **Tip** There is a more elegant Visual Basic programming construct called a control array that would produce equivalent results while reducing the amount of repetitive coding. The use of control arrays, however, would significantly increase the complexity of this project for the beginning programmer.

2 Close the Code window, and run and carefully test the program. All three reels should spin and then stop in left-to-right order, as indicated in the specifications. Make sure each reel's border appears when it stops, as shown in Figure 5.18.

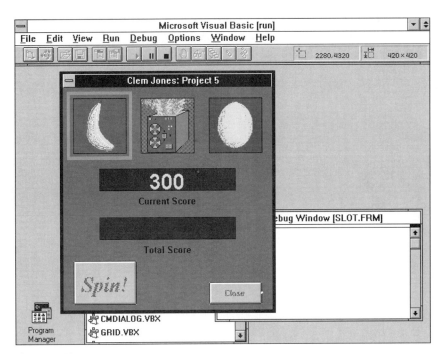

Figure 5.18

DISPLAYING THE CURRENT SCORE

Near the bottom of the timer event procedure, you will add code that calculates and displays the current score. Note that the current score can change on a subsequent call to the tmrSlot_Timer procedure if one or more of the reels has not yet stopped.

To display the current score:

1 Open the tmrSlot Code window.

2 Enter the following line of code after the last End If keyword to calculate the current score:

```
CurrentScore = (Reel1Stop + Reel2Stop + Reel3Stop) * 100
```

This is the sum of the three reel stop values multiplied by 100.

3 Enter the following line of code right after the code you entered in step 1:

```
lblCurrentScore.Caption = Format(CurrentScore, "##,##0")
```

The screen should resemble Figure 5.19.

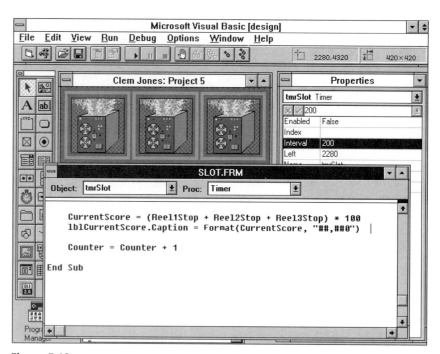

Figure 5.19

This line of code will display, with formatting, the current score as the caption of lblCurrentScore.

4 Close the Code window, and run and test the program.
The current score should fluctuate rapidly while the three reels change images. The result is shown in Figure 5.20.

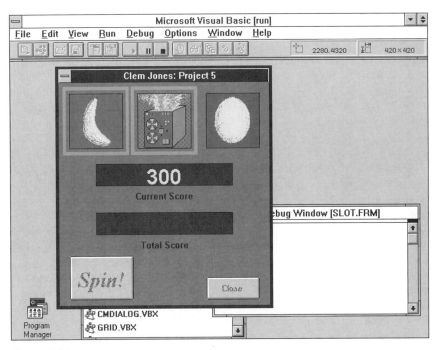

Figure 5.20

Controlling What Happens When the Timer Stops

When all three reels have stopped, several things should happen:

- The timer should stop ticking, since it won't be needed again until the user clicks the Spin button.
- The session total score should be incremented by the final value of the current score (and the updated session total value should be displayed).
- The Counter variable should be set to zero in preparation for another spin.
- The Spin and Close buttons should be enabled.

How can you determine when all of these steps execute? It is after the final reel has stopped: In other words, it is when the value of the Counter variable has exceeded 45.

To implement code for the timer:

1 Open the tmrSlot Code window, and enter the following code near the bottom of tmrSlot_Timer, replacing the line that reads *Counter = Counter + 1*:

```
If Counter >= 45 Then
  tmrSlot.Enabled = False
  Counter = 0
  SessionTotalScore = SessionTotalScore + CurrentScore
  lblSessionTotal.Caption = Format(SessionTotalScore,
  "##,##0")
  CurrentScore = 0
  cmdSpin.Enabled = True
  cmdClose.Enabled = True
Else
  Counter = Counter + 1
End If
```

Notice that the increment of Counter has been moved to the Else clause of the If statement.

2 Close the Code window, and run and test the program.

When the reels stop spinning, the screen should resemble Figure 5.21. Notice that the border shapes around each reel remain visible after the initial spin. They should disappear when you click the Spin button. You should be able to start the reels spinning again by clicking the Spin button.

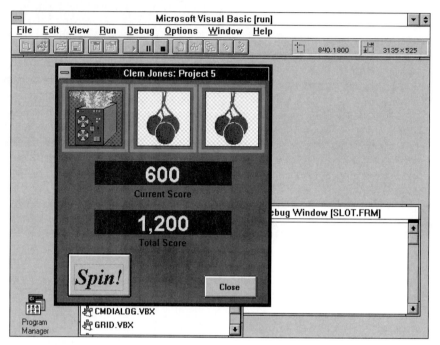

Figure 5.21

3 Stop the program.

In the steps that follow, you will modify the code for cmdSpin_Click so that the Visible property for the three border shapes is set to False.

To erase the border shapes when the Spin button is selected:

1 Open the cmdSpin_Click procedure, and modify the code to read as follows:

```
shpReel1Border.Visible = False
shpReel2Border.Visible = False
shpReel3Border.Visible = False
tmrSlot.Enabled = True
cmdSpin.Enabled = False
cmdClose.Enabled = False
```

2 Close the Code window, and run the program again.

3 Thoroughly test the program to ensure that all of the event procedures are working correctly.

Notice that the border shapes disappear each time you click the Spin button. Check out the three cherries in Figure 5.22!

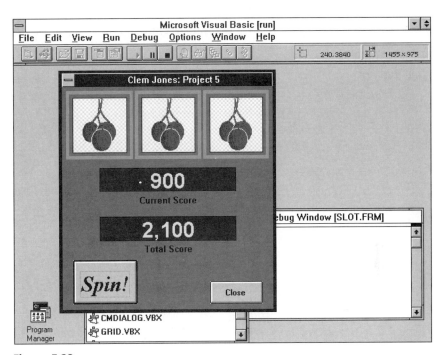

Figure 5.22

4 Save the program.

THE NEXT STEP

The slot machine you are creating is starting to develop into a decent Windows application. You have investigated the use of Image, Shape and Timer controls and have used the function Rnd and Randomize statement to create random numbers. You have also looked at the lifetime of different types of variables, an important concept for programmers to understand. The ease with which graphics can be manipulated with Visual Basic opens the door to numerous possibilities. Visual Basic is often used as a multimedia development tool because of its effortless interaction with various graphics elements, sound, and music.

In Project 6, you will improve the slot machine, adding a complete menu system and an About box. You will also use another Visual Basic file type, the Code module.

This concludes Project 5. You can either exit Visual Basic or go on to work the Study Questions, Review Exercises, and Assignments.

SUMMARY AND EXERCISES

Summary

- The Image control is used to display a bitmap image, or picture.
- The Shape control allows you to display simple graphical objects like rectangles, ovals, and rounded rectangles.
- The Timer control responds to the passage of time and generates a timer event message at specific intervals.
- The lifetime of a variable is determined by the way that variable is declared.
- A variable declared with Dim has the same lifetime as the procedure that the variable was declared within; a variable declared with Static persists for the entire program.
- The Rnd function is used to create random numbers.
- The Randomize statement initializes the random number generator in Visual Basic.

Key Terms and Operations

Key Terms

Image control
lifetime
Randomize statement
Rnd function
Shape control
Static statement
Timer control
timer event message
timer event procedure

Operations

Create random numbers
Use image controls
Use shape controls
Use timer controls

Study Questions

Multiple Choice

1. Which control is used to display a bitmap picture?
   a. Timer
   b. BitMap
   c. Frame
   d. Image
   e. Text Box

2. Which control is used to display simple shapes like rectangles and circles?
   a. Image
   b. Shape
   c. Form
   d. Square
   e. Picture

3. The Timer control responds to what event?
   a. time   passage of time
   b. date
   c. right clicking
   d. selection
   e. highlighting

4. Which property is used to specify the number of milliseconds that pass between one Timer event and the next?
   a. Time
   b. Timer
   c. Passage
   d. Interval
   e. msec

5. The Timer control is
   a. not very accurate.
   b. extremely accurate.
   c. accurate unless your program is graphics-intensive.
   d. accurate enough to be used in critical applications.
   e. not even close to an actual timer.

6. An interval setting of 300 would result in a timer event roughly how often?
   a. every .03 second
   b. every .02 second
   c. every .1 second
   d. every .003 second   .3
   e. every 3 seconds

7. The lifetime of a variable declared with the Dim keyword is
   a. the duration of the entire program.
   b. the duration of the procedure the variable is declared within.
   c. determined by the Timer control.
   d. can be set by the programmer to be any value.
   e. static.

8. Variables declared with the Static keyword
   a. retain their values even when the procedure they are declared within ends.
   b. retain their values even after the program they are within is ended.
   c. retain their values for the duration of the procedure they are declared within.
   d. retain their values until the Reset statement is executed.
   e. retain their values for a length of time determined by the Duration property.

9. The lifetime of a Static variable is
   a. forever.
   b. the duration of the procedure the variable is declared within.
   c. the duration of the entire program.
   d. determined by the Timer control.
   e. is preset by Visual Basic but can be modified by the programmer.

10. Random numbers in Visual Basic are created with
    a. Rnd and Randomize.
    b. Rnd and Seed.
    c. Randomize and Seed.
    d. Timer and Rnd.
    e. Rnd, Randomize, and Seed.

Short Answer

1. What is an Image control used to display?

2. What property would you use to make an Image control "invisible"?

3. Can the Shape control be used to display 3D objects?

4. What are some of the shapes that a Shape control can be?

5. What type of message does the Timer control send at specific intervals?

6. What does a variable's lifetime describe?

7. How would you declare a variable named MyVar that you wanted to persist for the entire program?

8. What range can a number returned by Rnd be within?

9. Why must the Randomize statement be used before a random number is generated?

10. Can a computer generate a truly random number?

For Discussion

1. Static variables retain their values even when the procedure they are declared in is ended. How would you reset a Static variable to zero?

2. Causing periodic code execution is one of the more powerful ways to use the Timer control. Can you think of any other areas where the Timer control might be useful?

3. John Von Neumann asserted that generating truly random numbers using arithmetical methods was impossible. Was he right? Why?

Review Exercises

Creating a PIN Generator

Banks typically assign a randomly generated Personal Identification Number (PIN) to each new Automated Teller Machine (ATM) card that they dispense. Using Figure 5.23 as a guide, write a Visual Basic program that will generate four random numbers when the user presses the Generate button.

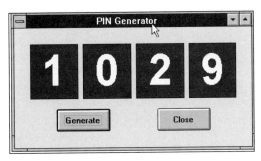

Figure 5.23

Developing a WingDings Slot Machine

Windows includes a standard TrueType font called WingDings, which, instead of letters of the alphabet and punctuation, contains various decorative typographic symbols (called wingdings or dingbats). For example, if you are using the WingDings font, typing a capital *J* will actually display a happy face; typing a percent sign (%) will display a bell; typing a capital *T* will display a snowflake; typing a capital *M* will display a bomb. You can experiment with the WingDings font by using Word or the Character Map accessory.

Using the slot machine files you created in this project, create a pair of new files (WSLOT.MAK, WSLOT.FRM). Instead of bitmap images, use single-character labels (in the WingDings font). Choose a large point size, center alignment, and your favorite foreground and background colors.

Assignments

Upgrading the PIN Generator

Modify the PIN generator from the first review exercise in this project by having each number cycle through a randomly generated list of numbers. The numbers should be generated one at a time. That is, when the user presses the Generate button, the first label should cycle through a list of numbers before settling on one after a set period of time. Then the second label should start cycling through a list of random numbers, and so on. You will recognize that this program has several features in common with the slot machine.

Creating a More Realistic Slot Machine

Using the slot machine files you created in this project, create a pair of new files (RSLOT.MAK, RSLOT.FRM). Change the scoring system so that each spin involves an automatic bet of one dollar and so that only certain combinations of images (for example, three cherries) yield a payoff. It will therefore be possible for the session total score to become a negative number. You can presume that the user has infinitely deep pockets (this is not the more realistic part).

Here is a suggested payoff system:

3 cherries pay $50

2 cherries pay $5

3 of a kind (lemon, banana, computer) pay $25

2 of a kind (lemon, banana, computer) pay $1

All other combinations cause the total score to be reduced by $1 (that is, they "pay" $-1).

Developing a Counting Tutor

Referring to Figure 5.24 and to the description of the Wingdings font in the second review exercise, create a simple counting tutor program for small children. Choose a Wingding symbol such as the snowflake. The program should display, in a label, a random number of snowflakes (between 1 and 9). The user should be able to type a number into a text box to indicate how many snowflakes are visible. If the number typed is correct, another random number of snowflakes is displayed; otherwise, the user will have to try again. The user will be able to type in answers until the correct answer is achieved.

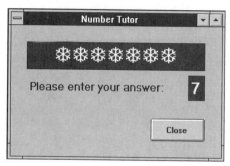

Figure 5.24

Objectives

After completing this project, you should be able to:

▶ Add menus to a Visual Basic program

▶ Use the Menu Design window

▶ Enable and disable menu items

▶ Add a second form to a Visual Basic program

▶ Assign events to menu items

▶ Add a code module to a project

▶ Program an About box

▶ Control the focus between different forms

▶ Create animation using the Move method

CASE STUDY: IMPROVING THE SLOT MACHINE

The slot machine program that you began in Project 5 is close to being a full-fledged Windows program. With only a few improvements, the slot machine can be made into a program you will be proud to put next to Solitaire and Minesweeper. These improvements include menus and an About box, features that all good Windows programs should include. It will also include some animation: When the program ends, all of the controls will fly right off the form.

Designing the Solution

In this project you will enhance the slot machine program you created in Project 5 with the addition of a menu, an About box, and some animation. These features are designed to give your application a more polished, professional look and will increase the usability of the slot machine.

The specifications for this program are as follows:

■ The same form and MAK file from Project 5 should be used, with the addition of a menu bar. The main program should otherwise operate in the same manner as the one you created in Project 5.

■ The menu bar should include File, Game, and Help selections.

- The File menu should have a New option that will restart the game and an Exit option that allows the user to end the program. The Exit option should duplicate the action of cmdClose.
- The Game menu should have a Spin option that duplicates the action of cmdSpin.
- The Help menu should include an About Slot Machine selection that will activate an About box containing project and programmer information. The user should not be able to switch back to the slot machine program until the OK button on the About box is pressed.

Using the OPE Flowchart

Figure 6.1 shows the flowchart for the project. You will make extensive use of this flowchart when building the program.

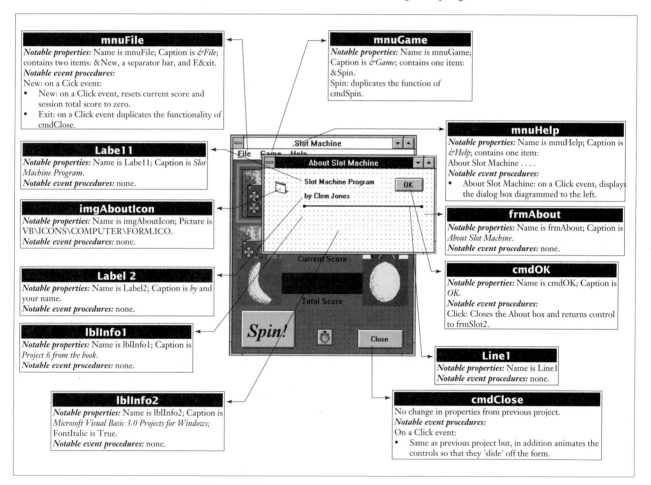

Figure 6.1

Because the Project 5 form and MAK file will comprise the basis of this project, you should load Project 5 into Visual Basic and resave the form and project files with new names.

To save form and project files under new names:

1 Start Visual Basic if you have not already done so.

2 Open SLOT.MAK and save the project as SLOT2.MAK.

3 Save SLOT.FRM as SLOT2.FRM.

4 Change the form caption to show that the current project is Project 6.

DESIGNING MENUS WITH VISUAL BASIC

Visual Basic has a tool, the **Menu Design Window**, that makes creating menuing systems quick and easy from within the Visual Basic environment. This Window is accessed by pressing the Menu Design Window button on the toolbar or by selecting Menu Design from the Window menu. The Menu Design Window is shown in Figure 6.2.

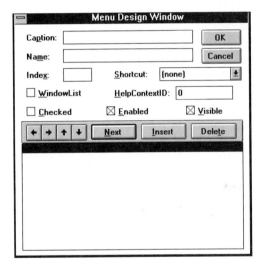

Figure 6.2

The various tools on the Menu Design Window, as shown in Figure 6.2, facilitate the creation of powerful menu systems. Creating a menu involves creating *Menu controls* and assigning properties to those controls. A **Menu control**, similar to other controls, is an object that defines a menu selection.

There are various types of menus. The menu system you will design for the slot machine program is called a drop-down, or pull-down, menu. It is the most common type of menu and will act similar to the menus in Visual Basic, Word, or Excel.

Using the Menu Design Window

You will now add a drop-down menu to the slot machine program. The menu should have three *titles*, or main selections, and each of these selections will have choices or options. The slot machine program will have three menu titles: File, Game, and Help. Menu titles will typically have a letter that is underlined. This underlined letter designates the *access key*, which is used in conjunction with (ALT) to allow the menu option to be accessed from the keyboard.

To create a menu system with the Menu Design Window:

1 Click the Menu Design Window button.
The Menu Design window appears.

2 Type **&File** for the **Caption** property, press (TAB), and type **mnuFile** for the **Name** property.
The access key is set to F. When your program runs, the user will be able to select the File menu by pressing (ALT)+F or by using the mouse.

> **Reminder** The ampersand, &, is used to determine the access key for a menu selection.

3 Select **Next** to design the next menu title.

4 Type **&Game** for the **Caption** property and **mnuGame** for the **Name** property.

5 Select **Next**, type **&Help** for the **Caption** property and **mnuHelp** for the **Name** property.

6 Close the Menu Design Window.

7 Run the program.
The screen should resemble Figure 6.3. Your program will have a menu bar and three menu titles: File, Game, and ~~About~~. They do not do anything yet, and no menus appear when you click the menu titles.

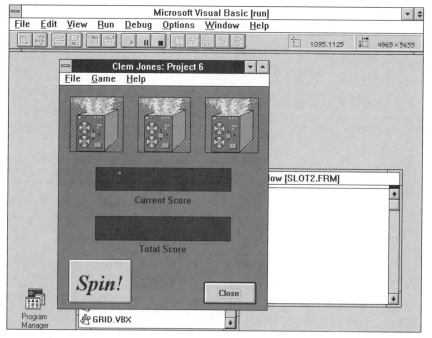

Figure 6.3

8 Stop the program.

Adding Options to the Menu Titles

Obviously, a menu bar isn't much good without the actual menus. Menus will appear under menu titles only when there are menu options to display. You will again use the Menu Design window to design these options.

 ### To add options to the File menu:

1 Open the Menu Design Window.

2 Select **&Game** in the Menu Control list box, as shown in Figure 6.4.

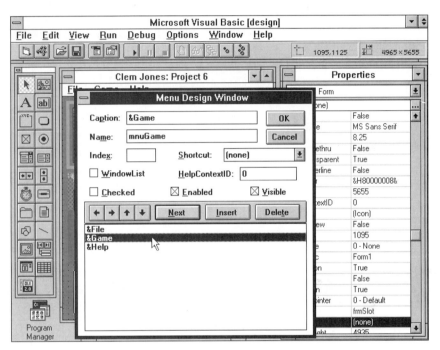

Figure 6.4

3 Click the Insert button to add a menu option.

Note that the option you will add will be placed under the File menu. Clicking Insert made room to add a menu title or option between File and Game, as shown in Figure 6.5.

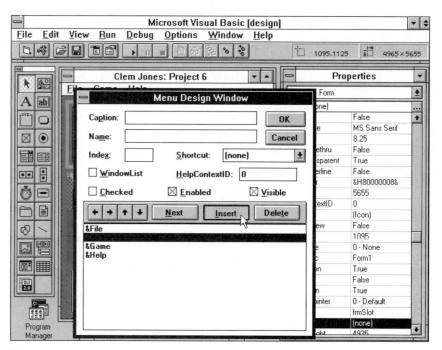

Figure 6.5

4 Click the right arrow button to indicate that the option you are creating will be indented.

This indentation will cause the menu item you are creating to be an option below the previous menu item. In other words, the menu item you are creating will be part of the File menu. Notice that four periods (....) appear in the Menu Control list box, as shown in Figure 6.6.

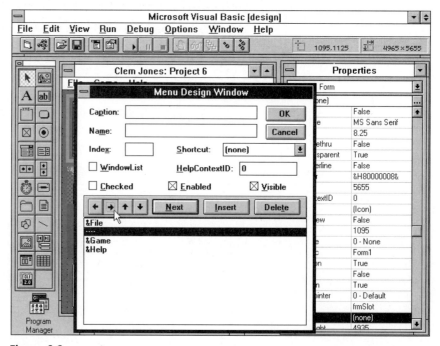

Figure 6.6

5 Type **&New** for the **Caption** property and **mnuFileNew** for the **Name** property.

6 Click the Insert button to insert a blank space between &New and &Game.

7 Press the right arrow button and type – (a hyphen) for the **Caption** property and **mnuFileSeparatorBar** for the **Name** property.

Using a hyphen for the caption causes the Menu Design Window to create a separator bar, which separates menu items into like categories. Since the New option and the Exit option do two different actions, you will use the separator bar to segregate them visually.

8 Insert a blank space between the separator bar and &Game, and then type **E&xit** for the **Caption** property and **mnuFileExit** for the **Name** property.

To add options to the Game and Help menus:

1 Using techniques similar to the previous steps, add an option to the Game menu, typing **&Spin** as the caption and **mnuGameSpin** as the name.

2 Add an option below Help. Type **&About Slot Machine...** for the caption and **mnuHelpAbout** for the name.

The Menu Design Window should now resemble Figure 6.7. Note that the ellipses (...) used in the caption indicates that selecting the option will cause a *dialog box* to open. Dialog boxes are used to display information to the user. Using an ellipses in a menu item is a Windows convention that indicates a dialog box will open when that item is selected.

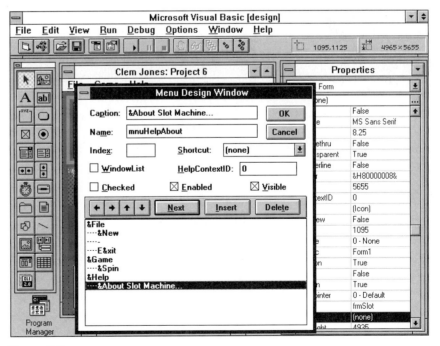

Figure 6.7

3 Select OK to exit the Menu Design Window.

WRITING CODE FOR MENUS

When a menu item is chosen by the user, a click event is generated. This should be a familiar concept to you by now, so it will be unsurprising that writing code for a menu will involve opening a Code window for a menu click procedure and adding the pertinent code.

Adding Code to the Menu

The Spin and Exit menu options are supposed to duplicate the functions of the Spin and Close command buttons. This can be achieved by calling the corresponding command button Click event procedures from the menu selection Code windows. In other words, the mnuGameSpin Click event procedure will do nothing more than call the cmdSpin Click event procedure. The mnuFileExit Click event procedure will, in turn, call cmdClose's Click event procedure. This saves a lot of typing, but the real benefit is that code is not duplicated in two different procedures.

First, you will need to add a few lines of code to the cmdSpin and cmdClose Click event procedures.

The cmdSpin Click event procedure, as shown in Figure 6.8, sets the Spin and Exit buttons Enabled properties to False while the reels are spinning.

Figure 6.8

Since the Spin and Exit menu options are duplicating the functions of the Spin and Close buttons, their Enabled properties will need to be set to False as well.

To adapt the cmdSpin Click event procedure:

1 Open the Code window for cmdSpin.

2 Enter the following lines of code at the end of the procedure, right before the End Sub:

```
mnuGameSpin.Enabled = False
mnuFileNew.Enabled = False
mnuFileExit.Enabled = False
```

3 Close the Code window.

To add code to the mnuFileSpin Click event procedure:

1 Open the mnuGameSpin Code window by selecting **Game** and then **Spin** from the menu bar on your form.
Note that you select the menu options as if you were using the program; when you release the mouse button on a menu option, that option's Code window opens.

> **Reminder** Opening the Code window for a menu item involves only selecting that menu item with the cursor. This is different than opening the Code window for other controls, where you must double-click on the control to open a Code window.

2 Type the following line of code in mnuGameSpin_Click:

```
cmdSpin_Click
```

3 Close the Code window.
The next step will be to add code to the mnuFileExit Click event procedure.

To add code to the mnuFileExit Click event procedure:

1 Open the mnuFileExit Code window by selecting **File** and then **Exit** from the menu bar on your form.

2 Type **cmdClose_Click** inside the procedure.

3 Close the Code window.

There is just one more adjustment that you need to make. You will recall that the tmrSlot_Timer procedure re-enables the Spin and Close buttons when 45 clicks have passed. You will also need this procedure to re-enable the menu selections for Spin, New, and Exit.

To add code to the tmrSlot_Timer procedure:

1 Open the Code window for tmrSlot, and enter the following lines of code below the line that reads *cmdSpin.Enabled = True*:

```
mnuGameSpin.Enabled = True
mnuFileNew.Enabled  = True
mnuFileExit.Enabled = True
```

2 Close the Code window, and run the program a couple of times to test the Spin and Exit menu options as shown in Figure 6.9. Notice that they provide the same functions as the Spin and Close command buttons, because choosing the menu options calls the click event procedures for the corresponding command button. They also provide a simple way for the user to control the slot machine program using only the keyboard.

3 Try the keyboard equivalents for the menu items instead of using the mouse as shown in Figure 6.9.

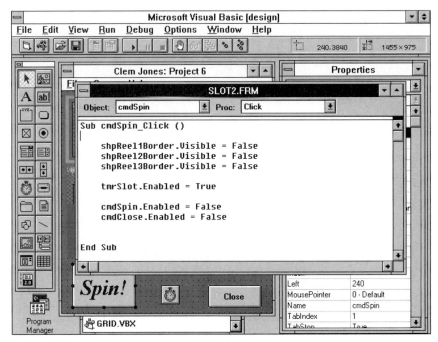

Figure 6.9

4 Stop the program.

 If necessary, you can save your work, exit Visual Basic, and continue this project later.

Adding Code to the New Menu Option

The menu option mnuFileNew will cause the game to reset, setting the current score and the total score to zero. Adding code to accomplish this is similar to the other menu coding you have done up to this point.

To add code to the New menu option:

1 Select **File** and then **New** from the menu bar on frmSlot2. This causes the Code window for mnuFileNew to open.

2 Add the following lines of code to mnuFileNew_Click:

```
lblCurrentScore.Caption = ""
lblSessionTotal.Caption = ""
```

3 Close the Code window, and run the program.

Pay special attention to the New option in the File menu. While the New option does initially blank out lblCurrentScore and lblSessionTotal, a few sample runs will show that SessionTotalScore is not actually reset to zero. Every time the session total score is shown, the score retains its previous value and adds the current score to obtain the new total score.

DETERMINING THE SCOPE OF A VARIABLE

You will recall that the lifetime of a variable affects the duration of time that a variable can retain its value. Because SessionTotalScore is declared as Static, it can "remember" its value even though the procedure it is declared in is run and exited repeatedly throughout the course of the program's execution.

SessionTotalScore, like all variables, is only visible from its own procedure. This visibility is called a variable's *scope*. The variable SessionTotalScore cannot be accessed from any procedure other than tmrSlot_Timer; that is its scope. It would be handy to be able to set SessionTotalScore to zero from mnuFileNew_Click. This would solve the problem nicely, but because SessionTotalScore's scope is limited to tmrSlot_Timer, such code would only generate an error.

Declaring Global Variables

Declaring a variable with Dim or Static automatically sets that variable's scope to the procedure it is declared within. If you would like to have a variable accessible from more than one procedure, you can declare it as a *Global variable*. A Global variable has a scope, or visibility, of the entire program; it can be accessed by any procedure in your project. A Global variable, like a Static variable, also has a lifetime of the entire program execution. Global variables do not lose their values when a particular procedure ends.

Global variables are declared in a similar manner to other variables, with the keyword Global replacing Dim or Static. Some examples of legal Global variable declarations are

```
Global MyVariable As Single
Global Counter As Integer
```

Because Global variables are so unique and should be accessible to every procedure, they need to be declared outside of any form. Visual Basic provides a handy place to declare global variables: the *code module*.

Adding a Code Module

A *code module* is like a form with no visual element. It can contain variable and constant declarations and Visual Basic code. A code module is a separate file that ends in a *BAS* extension.

To add a code module to your project:

1 Select **File** and **New Module** from the Visual Basic menu. The Code window for the new code module opens with the name **Module1.bas.**

2 Select **File** and **Save File As**.

3 Type **SLOT2.BAS** as the **Name** property of the new code module.

4 Below the words *Option Explicit*, add the following line of code:

```
Global SessionTotalScore As Single
```

The code *Option Explicit* ensures that variables must be declared before they are used. If you make a typing error when keying in variable names, the compiler can warn you if you try to access a variable that hasn't been declared.

5 Close SLOT2.BAS, and open the Code window for tmrSlot_Timer.

6 Change the line of code that reads

```
Static CurrentScore, SessionTotalScore As Integer
```

to

```
Static CurrentScore As Integer
```

7 Close the Code window, and run the program. Test the Spin option again, checking to see that your new global variable is doing its job.

8 Stop the program.

PROGRAMMING AN ABOUT BOX

Most Windows programs include an About box in the Help menu. The About box is used to display information about the program. There is usually copyright information as well as the release date and version number. You will not be copyrighting the slot machine program, but you will include information for your instructor that was previously included in the main form caption.

Since this program will most resemble a typical Windows application, the first step is to change the caption on frmSlot.

To change the frmSlot caption:

1 Select frmSlot by clicking any blank area on the form.

2 Type **Slot Machine** as the **Caption** property.

Creating a Second Form

So far you have been working with only one form per Visual Basic project. This does not have to be the case; in fact, most Visual Basic programs use several forms. Because the About box is a separate window, it will require its own form.

To create a new form:

1 Select **File** and **New Form** from the Visual Basic menu.

2 Resize the form, and change the properties as listed in Figure 6.1.

3 Using Figure 6.1 as a guide, add the imgAboutIcon and cmdOK controls to the new form.

4 Assign the properties for these controls as they are specified in the flowchart.

The screen should now resemble Figure 6.10

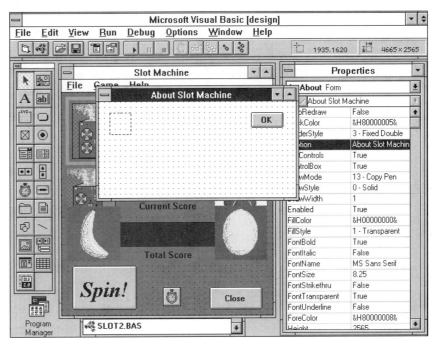

Figure 6.10

Adding an Icon to the About Box

Following traditional Windows application practice, your About box should include an icon that matches the icon the program will use if it is placed in a Program Manager group. Icons are special graphic bitmap files that have the extension .ICO. In this case the icon is called FORM.ICO, and it is normally located in the VB\ICONS\COMPUTER directory.

To add an icon to the About box, you will use the Image control that you placed on the form earlier. Remember that an Image control is used to hold bitmap images, including icon images.

To add an icon to imgAboutIcon:

1 Double-click the **Picture** property of imgAboutIcon to open the Load Picture dialog box.

2 Select the ICONS directory and the COMPUTER directory.

3 Double-click FORM.ICO to load it into the Image control. If your computer does not have FORM.ICO, you can you use any bitmap graphics file instead. The Load Picture dialog box will close, and the screen should now resemble Figure 6.11. That's it! You've added an icon to your About box.

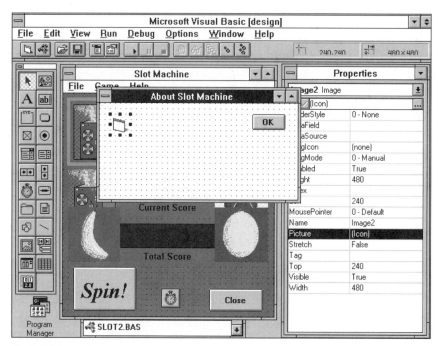

Figure 6.11

Adding Labels to the About Box

You need to add a couple of labels to the About box. You will be using the About box primarily to display information about yourself and the project.

To add labels to frmAbout:

1 Using Figure 6.1 as a guide, create Label1 and Label2.

2 Assign the properties listed in the flowchart to the two labels so that the screen resembles Figure 6.12.

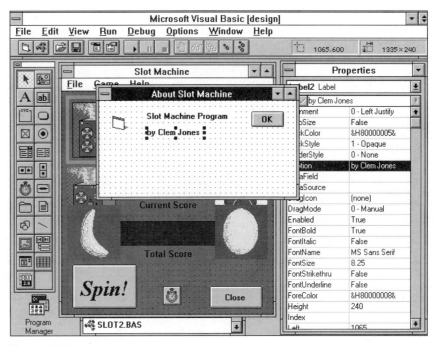

Figure 6.12

Using the Line Tool

The *Line tool* offers a simple way to draw straight lines directly on a form. Most About boxes use a straight line to separate information logically.

To add a Line control to frmAbout:

1 Select the **Line tool** from the Toolbox.

2 Using Figure 6.13 as a guide, draw a horizontal straight line on the About box.

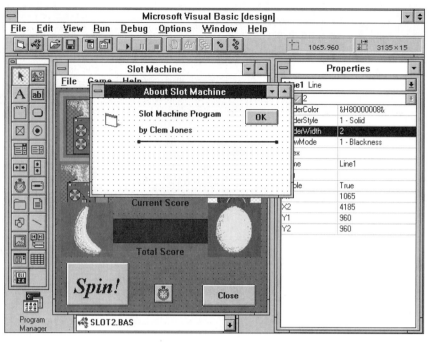

Figure 6.13

Completing the Visual Design of the About Box

According to the flowchart, you need to add two more Label controls to the About box. These labels display information about the project. The text that is entered in the second label is longer than other text you have used and will demonstrate a feature of the Label control called *text wrap*. Similar to a word processor, Label controls automatically wrap text to the next line when the text is too long to fit on the current line.

To create the other labels for frmAbout:

1 Using Figure 6.1 as a guide, create lblInfo1 and lblInfo2.

2 Again using the flowchart, change the properties for the two new labels.

The screen should now resemble Figure 6.14.

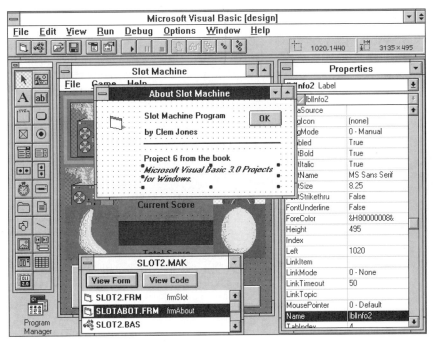

Figure 6.14

3 Save and run the program.
Nothing happens if you select About Slot Machine from the Help menu because you have not yet added any code to access the About box.

4 Stop the program.

Adding Code to the About Slot Machine Menu Option

Before you can access the About box, you need to write code to do so in the mnuHelpAbout Click event procedure. When a user accesses an About box in a Windows program, the form's Main window is unavailable until the user selects the OK button in the About box. This is called controlling the focus. An About box should have the focus until it is closed. During the time the About box has the focus, the other form should be unavailable. Your program will include this behavior by using the Enabled property to disable frmSlot when the user selects the About Slot Machine option.

At the same time, you will set the Enabled property of frmAbout to True, enabling frmAbout. You will also set the Visible property of frmAbout to True, making the About box appear on-screen.

 To add code to the mnuHelpAbout click event procedure:

1 Open the Code window for mnuHelpAbout by selecting **Help** and then **About** from the menu on the slot machine form.

2 Add the following code to the click event procedure:

```
frmSlot.Enabled = False
frmAbout.Enabled = True
frmAbout.Visible = True
```

3 Close the Code window.

Adding Code to the OK Button

When the OK button in the About box is pressed, the inverse should occur: frmSlot should be enabled, and the frmAbout properties Enabled and Visible should both be set to False. This code will be entered in the cmdOK click event procedure.

To add code to the cmdOK click event procedure:

1 Open the Code window for cmdOK.

2 Add the following code to the click event procedure:

```
frmAbout.Enabled = False
frmAbout.Visible = False
frmSlot.Enabled = True
frmSlot.SetFocus
```

3 Close the Code window.

4 Run the program, and select **About Slot Machine** from the **Help** menu.

Notice that when you try to click frmSlot, the computer beeps at you. The program will not allow you to access the form's Main window until you close the About box. Figure 6.15 shows the final About box in action.

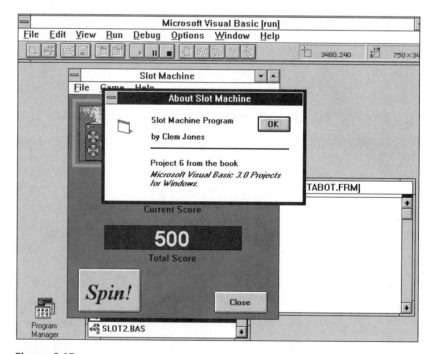

Figure 6.15

5 Stop the program.

 If necessary, you can save your work, exit Visual Basic, and continue this project later.

ADDING ANIMATION

At this point, the slot machine is a fully functioning Windows program with menus and an About box. The only remaining step to make it conform to specifications is to have the controls slide off the form when the user clicks the Close button. Visual Basic provides various ways to achieve this type of animation. The easiest is the *Move method.*

Using the Move Method to Animate Controls

The **Move method** can be used to move controls across the surface of the form. The controls are not visible if you attempt to display them outside of the boundaries of the form, so by moving the controls toward the edge of the form, they seem to disappear.

Move takes two basic arguments that determine the new left and top coordinates of a control. The current left and top coordinates, should you need to use them, can be found in the Left and Top properties for that object. Motion can be created by repositioning the object's current coordinates.

> **Tip** Screen measurements in Visual Basic are usually measured in **twips**, a unit that is 1/1440 of an inch or 1/20 of a typographic point. Moving a control within a form is always relative to the origin (0,0), which is located in the upper-left corner of the form.

The syntax of the Move method is as follows:

```
object.Move left, top
```

where *object* is the name of the control you will be repositioning, *left* is the value indicating the coordinate for the horizontal left edge of the object, and *top* is the vertical top edge coordinate of the object.

To make an object move off the screen, you will write code that will repeat a certain number of times until the object goes off the screen. Such repetition requires the use of the *For-Next statement.*

Using the For-Next Statement in a Move

Programs frequently need to execute a group of instructions repeatedly. This is called **iteration** or **looping.** The **For-Next statement** is a type of loop used to repeat an instruction or series of instructions a specific number of times. The code between the For and Next keywords is the **body** of the loop. A **counter**, or loop control variable, is used to keep track of how many times the loop has executed. This counter variable is automatically **incremented** (increased by one) each time the loop is completed.

In the code you'll be writing for the Move method, it is necessary to move the control from its origin point to a location somewhere outside of the form. This is what creates the animation effect, and it is easily achieved using a For-Next loop.

The For-Next loop you will be using will be similar to

```
For I = 1 To 50
Move the object down one unit
Next
```

In this case the loop will execute 50 times, and each time it executes, the object will move down a little bit on the form. Because the loop repeats over and over until the incremental variable *I* is equal to 50, the control moves across the form smoothly.

The first step will be to add some animation to one control to get a feel for how it works. Then adding the animation to the other controls will be a simple matter of reusing the code you will develop now.

Animating the Spin Button

To animate the Spin button:

1 Open the Code window for cmdClose, and type the following code before the End statement:

```
Dim I As Integer              ' I is an incremental variable
shpReel1Border.Visible = False
shpReel2Border.Visible = False
shpReel3Border.Visible = False

For I = 1 To 50
  cmdSpin.Move cmdSpin.Left, cmdSpin.Top + I
Next
```

The variable I is frequently used by programmers for use in repetitive loops: it stands for increment. You could choose any valid variable name, however; X, Count, and Counter are examples of other common variable names used for this purpose.

2 Close the Code window and run the program.

3 Click the Close button.

The Spin button should appear to fall off the window. Faster machines, especially, will produce smooth animation as the control moves.

Improving the Animation

Currently, the button falls straight down at a constant rate. It would be more interesting if it drifted to one side as it fell. This can be accomplished with a "push" variable that will randomly move the control to one side as it falls. Also, the speed of the control should increase as it falls, simulating the effects of gravity. To accelerate the button as it falls, you can square the value of the variable I and add that value to the top coordinate.

To add a gravitational effect to the animation:

1 Modify the code for cmdClose so that it resembles the following:

```
Dim I As Integer
Dim Push As Integer
shpReel1Border.Visible = False
shpReel2Border.Visible = False
shpReel3Border.Visible = False

Push = Int(Rnd * 20)
For I = 1 To 50
cmdSpin.Move cmdSpin.Left + Push, cmdSpin.Top + I ^ 2
Next
```

2 Close the Code window, and run the program.

3 Click the Close button.

The Spin button should now fall slightly to the right and should accelerate as it falls.

Animating the Other Controls

Animating the other controls will now be straightforward. Each of the controls on the form should disappear from the form in a manner similar to the Spin button. Some controls will move up, and some will move down.

To animate the other controls:

1 Modify the cmdClose_Click procedure so that it contains the following code:

```
Dim I As Integer
 Dim Push As Integer
       Reel
   shpSlot1Border.Visible = False
       Reel
   shpSlot2Border.Visible = False
       Reel
   shpSlot3Border.Visible = False

   Push = Int(Rnd * 20)
   For I = 1 To 20
     lblSessionTotal.Move lblSessionTotal.Left + Push,
 lblSessionTotal.Top + I ^ 2
   Next

   Push = Int(Rnd * 20)
   For I = 1 To 50
     cmdSpin.Move cmdSpin.Left + Push, cmdSpin.Top + I ^ 2
   Next

   Push = Int(Rnd * 20)
   For I = 1 To 50
     lblCurrentScore.Move lblCurrentScore.Left - Push,
 lblCurrentScore.Top + I ^ 2
   Next

   Push = Int(Rnd * 20)
   For I = 1 To 50          Reel
     imgReel3.Move imgSlot3.Left + Push, imgReel3.Top + I ^ 2
   Next

   Push = Int(Rnd * 20)
   For I = 1 To 50       Reel
     imgReel1.Move imgSlot1.Left - Push, imgReel1.Top + I ^ 2
   Next

   Push = Int(Rnd * 20)
   For I = 1 To 50      Reel
     imgReel2.Move imgSlot2.Left + Push, imgReel2.Top + I ^ 2
   Next
```

```
Push = Int(Rnd * 20)
For I = 1 To 50
  lblCurrentDescription.Move lblCurrentDescription.Left -
Push, lblCurrentDescription.Top - I ^ 2
Next

Push = Int(Rnd * 20)
For I = 1 To 50
  lblSessionDescription.Move lblSessionDescription.Left -
Push, lblSessionDescription.Top - I ^ 2
Next

Push = Int(Rnd * 20) + 50
For I = 1 To 50
  cmdClose.Move cmdClose.Left - Push, cmdClose.Top - I ^ 2
Next

End
```

2 Close the Code window, save your work, and run the program. Figure 6.16 shows the final project in action.

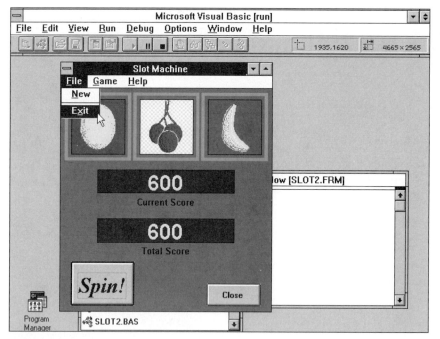

Figure 6.16

3 Try testing the Close button and the Exit selection from the File menu. You may want to play with the various values in the For-Next loops to achieve different animation effects.

THE NEXT STEP

You have now been introduced to some of Visual Basic's most exciting features and should be able to incorporate various controls, methods, and design techniques into future Windows programs that you create. An understanding of the menu design system and the concepts behind having multiple forms in a single project will provide useful insight into more powerful applications. You have also been exposed to some control animation using the Move command. The skills you have developed in this and previous projects can propel you to any future investigation of Visual Basic. How you choose to exercise these skills is up to you.

This concludes Project 6. You can either exit Visual Basic, or go on to work the Study Questions, Review Exercises, and Assignments.

SUMMARY AND EXERCISES

Summary

- The Menu Design Window is a powerful way to create menus with Visual Basic.
- Visual Basic projects are not limited to one form.
- An About box provides an elegant and consistent way to display program information to the user.
- Variables have scope, which determines the visibility of that variable.
- Global variables are visible to all procedures in a program and have the duration, or lifetime, of the program.
- Code modules can contain variable declarations and Visual Basic code.
- The Line tool can be used to separate information logically.
- Animation can be achieved in Visual Basic with the Move method.
- The For-Next statement provides a way to repeat a series of instructions by looping.

Key Terms and Operations

Key Terms

access key
body
code module
counter
dialog box
For-Next statement
Global variable
increment
iteration
Line tool
looping
Menu control
Menu Design Window

Move method
scope
text wrap
title
twip

Operations

Add a menu system to a project
Add a second form to a project
Create animation with the Move method
Control the focus
Use a code module to declare global variables

Study Questions

Multiple Choice

1. Menus are designed in Visual Basic with the
   a. Menu Designer.
   b. Menu Control list box.
   c. Menu Design Window.
   d. Menu Coder.
   e. Menu Wizard.

2. To create an access key for a menu item, which character is used?
   a. %
   b. *
   c. #
   d. &
   e.)

3. What is the prefix for a menu item?
   a. menu
   b. mn
   c. mnu
   d. gnu
   e. I

4. Menu items that cause a dialog box to open end in which characters?
   a. - - -
   b. :
   c. <d>
   d. ()
   e. ...

5. Opening the Code window for a menu item is different from opening the Code window for other controls because
   a. it requires only a single mouse click.
   b. the (CTRL) key must be held down to open it.
   c. you must enter the Code window from the Menu Design Window.
   d. menus items have two Code windows each.
   e. there is no Code window for a menu item.

6. An About box is used to
   a. display information about the program to the user.
   b. display personal information about the programmer.
   c. display the Help system.
   d. display an online version of the user's manual.
   e. quit the program.

7. The Line tool is used to
   a. draw straight and curved lines.
   b. draw straight lines.
   c. draw hollow squares.
   d. measure the distance, in twips, between two controls.
   e. underline text.

8. A code module can be used to
   a. replace a form graphically.
   b. declare Global variables.
   c. declare local variables that can be used in any procedure.
   d. hold graphics and code.
   e. contain all of the actual code for a Visual Basic project.

9. A variable's scope is the same as
   a. lifetime.
   b. duration.
   c. visibility.
   d. a code module.
   e. mouthwash.

10. Global variables can be declared
    a. in any procedure.
    b. on a form.
    c. in a code module.
    d. in a click event procedure.
    e. in a code event procedure.

Short Answer

1. What is the scope of a Global variable?

2. Is it possible to have more than one form in a Visual Basic program?

3. How do you add a code module to a project?

4. What method is used to animate controls?

5. The For-Next statement is an example of what type of construct?

For Discussion

1. What is the difference between lifetime and scope? Why are these concepts often confused?

2. Code modules are often used to declare Global variables. What else do you think a code module would be good for?

3. Most programs use more than one form or window. Besides an About box, what other additional forms would most Windows programs use?

4. Looping constructs are an important part of all programming languages because they allow a nonsequential execution of code. How are looping constructs implemented in Visual Basic?

Review Exercises

Creating a Hovering Greeting

Enhance the greeting program from Project 2 so that when the user clicks the Greeting button, lblHello hovers in a small region over txtInputName. You can accomplish this by using the Move method and making small random changes to the Left and Top properties of the label. Make sure the label won't drift entirely off the window. You will probably also want to make the form bigger and spread the controls out somewhat to allow for adequate movement of lblHello.

Improving the Loan Calculator

Improve the loan calculator from the review exercises in Project 4 by adding a menu system. The menu should include two items, Loan and Help. The Loan menu will have two options, New and Exit. New will set all text box values and corresponding variables to zero. Because of this, these variables will now need to be declared globally in a code module. The Exit option will duplicate the function of a Close button. The Help menu will have one item, Loan Calculator Help, which will open a second form. This second form will display brief descriptions of the various components of a loan: principle, interest rate, loan term, and monthly payment. It will also include an OK button. This help window should otherwise react in a similiar manner to an About box.

Creating a Reflex Game

Create the game Reflex shown in Figure 6.17. The picture of the face is created by using the Wingdings font and choosing the letter J as the caption. In Reflex the face command button is randomly placed on-screen every 750 milliseconds (use a Timer control for this). The player tries to click the face with the mouse. A click event on the command button causes the face to change to a happy face (letter K) briefly. When the player has successfully clicked the face 10 times, the game is over.

Figure 6.17

Assignments

Improving Reflex

Improve the Reflex game you created in the review exercise by constantly displaying the number of hits and by tracking the number of hits on the face versus the total number of times the command button is displayed. When the game is over (10 hits have been registered), display a label with a suitable message based on the accuracy of the player's game, as shown in Figure 6.18.

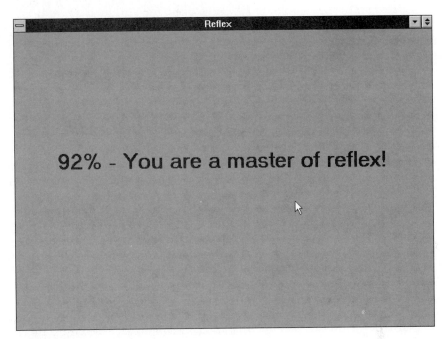

Figure 6.18

Here are some sample displays:

Percentage of Hits	Message
>= 90	You are a master of reflex!
80 - 89	You have excellent reflexes.
70 - 79	You have good reflexes.
60 - 69	You have average reflexes.
0 - 59	You have poor reflexes.

Creating an Airmail Game

Construct a game in which the player puts a "flying envelope" into a mailbox. The overall initial appearance of the game should resemble Figure 6.19.

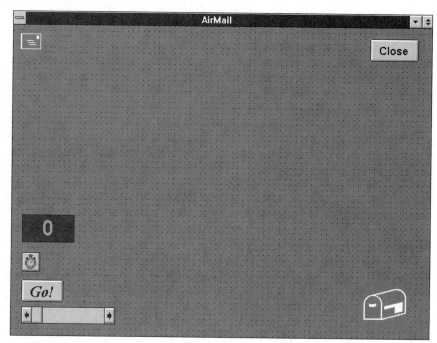

Figure 6.19

The various pictorial symbols in the game (a stamped envelope, various mailboxes) are all made from labels in the standard Windows TrueType WingDings font. The WingDings font characters show up as the following on the screen:

WingDings Character	On-screen Display
+	A picture of a stamped envelope
,	A closed mailbox, flag down
/	An open mailbox, flag down
.	An open mailbox, containing mail, flag up
-	A closed mailbox, flag up

The game works like this: When the user presses the Go command button, the timer is activated. The timer event procedure contains code that causes the the letter to fall a small amount downward on each timer tick. The mailbox opens (that is, its caption changes to /). The player uses the horizontal scroll bar to control the amount of "push" to the right or left.

Use the OPE chart in Figure 6.20 to construct the program. Note that you will need a module for the Global variable Friction. The acceptable range for a direct hit on the open mailbox will need some experimentation on your part. As noted in Figure 6.19, the only event procedures that need to have code are cmdClose_Click (which will contain just an End statement), cmdGo_Click, and tmrAnimator_Timer.

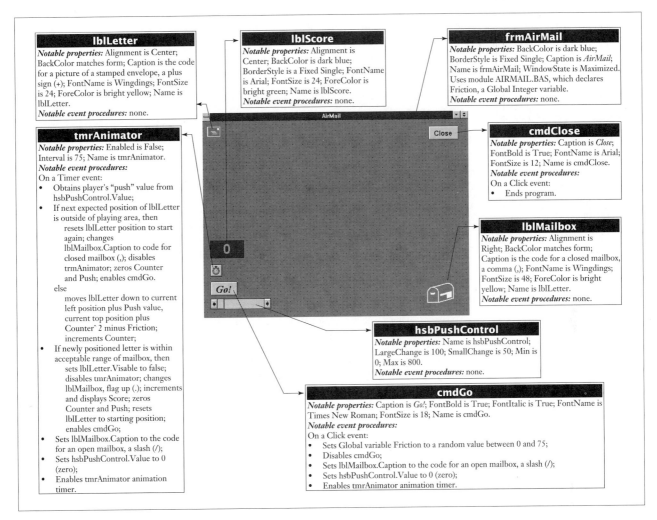

Figure 6.20

Adding Advanced Air Mail

Improve the mailbox game in Exercise 1 by adding a menu system and a randomly positioned mailbox. The visual style of the game will not change besides the addition of the menu.

The menu will have one item, Game, which should have three options, New, Go, and Exit. The New option will reset the score to zero, starting a new game. The Go option should duplicate the function of the Go command button. The Exit option will duplicate the function of cmdClose.

Use Rnd and Randomize to randomly place the mailbox at a different horizontal screen location at every "turn" so that the player cannot memorize a pattern.

Operations Reference

FILE

Button	Operation	Keystroke	Description
	New Project		Starts a new project.
	Open Project		Loads a previously saved project.
	Save Project		Saves the current project to disk.
	Save Project As		Saves the current project under a new name.
	New Form		Creates a new form for the current project.
	New MDI Form		Creates a multiple document interface window.
	Add file	(CONTROL) + D	Adds preexisting file to current project.
	Remove File		Removes a form or code module file from a project.
	New Module		Creates a new code module for the current project.
	Save File	(CONTROL) + S	Saves the active form or code module to disk.
	Save File As	(CONTROL) + A	Saves the active form or code module under a new name.
	Load text		Loads text files as code.
	Save Text		Saves code as a text file.
	Print	(CONTROL) + P	Prints the code, form, and/or the form text for the current form or for all forms.
	Make EXE File		Creates an executable file for the current project.
	Exit		Exits Microsoft Visual Basic.

EDIT

Button	Operation	Keystroke	Description
	Undo	(CONTROL) + Z	Undoes the previous action (not always possible).
	Redo		Repeats the previous action (not always possible).
	Cut	(CONTROL) + X	Removes the selected code or control and places it in the clipboard.
	Copy	(CONTROL) + C	Copies information to the clip board.
	Paste	(CONTROL) + V	Pastes information from the clipboard to a selection.
	Paste Link		Creates destination links that accept data from other applications.
	Delete	(DEL)	Deletes the selected code or control.
	Find	(CONTROL) + F	Performs a search for the specified text.
	Find Next	(F3)	Repeats the previous text search.
	Find Previous	(SHIFT) + (F3)	Repeats the previous text search; can be used in successive searches.
	Replace	(CONTROL) + R	Searches for and replaces the specified text.
	Bring to Front	(CONTROL) + =	Places selected control in front of others.
	Send to Back	(CONTROL) + −	Places selected control behind others.
	Align to Grid		Aligns a control to the form's preset grid.

VIEW

Button	Operation	Keystroke	Description
	Code	F7	Opens the code window for the currently selected object.
	New Procedure		Creates header for user-defined procedures.
	Next Procedure	CONTROL + ↓	Jumps to next procedure for currently selected object while in a code window.
	Previous Procedure	CONTROL + ↑	Jumps to previous procedure for currently selected object while in a code window.
	Procedure Definition	M + F2	Shows code for a procedure from a different procedure.
	Toolbar		Toggles the Toolbar window on and off.

RUN

Button	Operation	Keystroke	Description
▶	Start /Run	F5	Begin executing the current project.
■	End/Stop		End the current project.
	Restart	SHIFT + F5	Begins execution of current project.

OPTIONS

Button	Operation	Keystroke	Description
	Environment		Opens a dialog box that sets global Visual Basic options.
	Project		Opens a dialog box that sets options for the currently active project.

WINDOW

Button	Operation	Keystroke	Description
	Color Palette		Brings up color editing palate.
	Debug	CONTROL + B	Toggles debug windows on and off.
	Menu Design	CONTROL + M	Activates the Menu Design window, allowing a menu to be designed for the active project.
	Procedures	F2	Lists the procedures for an object.
	Project		Opens the Project window.
	Properties	F4	Opens the Properties window.
	Toolbox		Opens the Toolbox window.
	Data Manager		Allows creation of databases you can use with the data control.

HELP

Button	Operation	Keystroke	Description
	Contents		Displays the table of contents for the Help system
	Search For Help On		Displays an alphabetical index of Help topics that can easily be searched for key words.
	Obtaining Technical Support		Displays how to get Microsoft technical support for Visual Basic.
	Learning Microsoft Visual Basic		Provides an on-screen tutorial.
	About Microsoft Visual Basic		Displays copyright information about Microsoft Visual Basic.

TOOLBAR

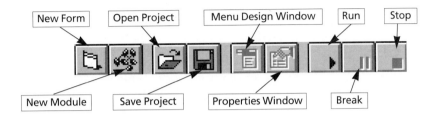

TOOLBOX

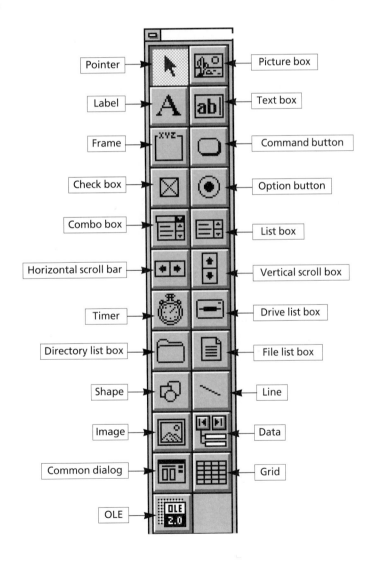

Glossary

access key The underlined letter in a menu title that determines the shortcut key that can be used to access that item. In the File menu for example, the F is underlined, so typing Alt-F would have the same effect as clicking File with the mouse.

Alignment property Property used to set the Alignment attribute of a font on a control or form.

argument the input for a function.

assignment operator The equal sign (=). When used in Visual Basic code, it usually means "calculate the value of whatever instructions are on the right hand side of the equal sign, and then store that value in the variable named on the left hand side of the equal sign."

BackColor property Property that sets the background color of a form and certain controls. The default value is white.

BAS file A code module.

BASIC (Beginners All-Purpose Instruction Code) A programming language developed in the late 1960ís by John Kemeny and Thomas Kurtz at Dartmouth College. Unlike the rather arcane computer languages that preceded it, BASIC was designed for non-programmers and it uses English-like source code that is easy to read and understand. Early versions of BASIC were interpreted because of the small memory sizes of the computers that were then available.

body The section of a For-Next statement between the For and Next keywords.

BorderColor property Property that sets the color of a shape or line control.

BorderStyle property Property used to set the border style on a form window. It has a small range of values, from 0-None to 3-Fixed Double.

BorderWidth property Property that determines the width of a shape or line control.

Cancel box A small button the Properties window that cancels the current entry in the Settings box and returns that setting to the previous entry if one exists. It resembles a small "X." It is the equivalent to hitting the Escape key.

Caption property A property that displays the caption for a particular control.

Change event An event that occurs when a control changes in some way. A Change event for a text box occurs when text is typed in by the user, for example.

Click event An event triggered by a mouse button click.

Click event procedure A procedure that is called in response to an Click Event.

code compatibility The ability of a programming language to generate source code that is compatible with another programming language. For example, most code written in QBASIC or QUICKBASIC is said to be code compatible with Visual Basic.

code module A special source code file that is like a form with no visual element. It can contain variable and constant declarations and Visual Basic code. A code module file ends in a BAS extension.

Code window The window in the Visual Basic IDE where code is entered by the programmer. The Code window can be opened by double clicking on any form or control, by choosing Code from the View menu, or by pressing F7 at any time.

command button Command buttons are used to provide the user with an easy way to cause an action to occur. Typical command buttons have captions like "OK," and "Cancel." When a command button is selected, it appears to be pushed in. Command buttons are sometimes called push buttons.

compiler A translator program that reads the source code all at once, generating a separate executable machine code file that can be directly understood and run by the computer. Compilers are like people who translate books into a new language: the book can then be read all at once, without the reader having to wait for the translator. Compiled code runs faster than interpreted code, but does not offer the benefits of immediate testing and partial execution.

Const statement Statement used to declare a constant.

constant A value that will not change for the "life" of the program. A constant is fixed, set in stone. Typical constants could include the value of Pi and the number of days in a week. Like variables, constants are named so they can be accessed from program code.

ControlBox property Property used to determine if a particular form will display a control menu box when the program it is contained within is run. It has only two settings, True and False.

controls The objects that provide the "look and feel" of a Visual Basic program. Controls define the visual front-end with which the user will interact. Objects like scroll bars, command buttons, and menus are all examples of controls.

counter A loop control variable used in a For-Next statement to keep track of how many times the loop has executed. This counter variable is automatically incremented each time the loop is completed.

data type The attribute of a variable which describes the category of data that the variable can contain. The data type of a variable determines the amount of memory needed for that variable to exist.

declare The act of enabling a variable by naming it and assigning a data type.

Dim statement Statement used to declare a variable. Dim is short for Dimension and is used in conjunction with the keyword As. The lifetime of a variable declared with Dim is the lifetime of the procedure in which it is declared.

Enabled property Property that determines the user's access to that control. It has two settings: True and False. If the Enabled property is set to True, the property is "on" and can be accessed by the user. If the Enabled property is "False," the property will appear grayed out and will not be accessible to the user.

End statement Statement that causes a Visual Basic program to cease execution.

Enter box A small button on the Properties window that accepts the current entry in the Settings box. It resembles a small check mark. It is the equivalent to hitting the Enter key.

event Any action that can be recognized by Windows and responded to appropriately. Mouse clicks, mouse movement, and a command button being pressed are all examples of events.

event driven programming A style of programming where a program spends most of its time waiting for events such as mouse clicks and text entry to occur. These events trigger certain lines of code which are designed to respond to these specific events.

Event procedure A procedure that is called in response to an Event.

EXE file An executable file that can be run natively in the Windows operating system. Visual Basic can generate executable files using the Make Exe option in the File menu.

Focus property Property that determines which object is the current, or selected, object. That is, the focus indicates where action will take place.

FontItalic property Property used to set the Italic attribute of a font on a control or form. The FontItalic property has two settings, True and False.

FontName property Property used to determine the font used with the currently selected control.

FontSize property Property used to set the size of the font on a control or form.

For-Next statement A type of loop used to repeat an instruction or series of instructions a specific number of times.

ForeColor property Property used to set the foreground color of a form and certain controls.

form A window.

form window The form window is the basis, or backdrop, of your program. Each project can have one or more forms. Controls are painted directly on the form window.

format function A function used to format, or punctuate, the output of a number, date, time, or string. The Format function uses a variety of special symbols to determine how the displayed value will look.

Frame control A control that is used to create logical groups of related controls. Frames have a border with a descriptive text title.

FRM file A form file.

function A special type of procedure that returns (sends back) a value. There are many functions built into the Visual Basic language. Functions can also be written by the programmer, similar in manner to writing an event procedure. A function takes arguments, which is the input for the function, and returns a value, which is the output. Because functions return a value, they can be used in larger expressions.

Global statement Statement used to declare a variable as globally visible. That is, the variable will be accessible to all procedures and modules in a program.

handles Small black boxes that appear around currently selected control that can be used to resize that control.

Horizontal Scroll Bar control Implementation of the horizontal variety of scroll bar. See scroll bar.

Hungarian naming convention Naming convention invented by Charles Simonyi where object names are given a descriptive prefix so that the meaning of the object is obvious. A form name in Visual Basic, for example, is preceded by the prefix frm.

IDE (Integrated Development Environment) A complete programming environment where all of the tools that a programmer requires to generate programs are housed in one convenient place. In the past programmers were forced to use separate tools to edit, compile, debug, and execute programs. Visual Basic allows you to perform all of these tasks without leaving the IDE.

If-Then-Else statement A statement that allows a Visual Basic program to execute certain lines of code, based on whether a certain condition is true. If the condition is true, the Then part of the statement is run. If the condition is false, the Else part is run.

Image control A control used to display a picture.

integer A data type used to store whole numbers.

interpreter A translator program that reads source code line-by-line as the program is executed, in the same way that a human interpreter translates words spoken in a foreign language as they are spoken. Generally, using an interpreter is slower than running a compiled program although interpreted programming languages offer the benefit of immediate testing and partial execution.

Interval property Timer property that specifies the number of milliseconds (1 millisecond = 1/1000 or 0.001 second) that pass between one timer event and the next. The interval must be between 0 and 64,767 inclusive. Since 64,767 milliseconds translates to roughly 65 seconds, every thousand milliseconds is one second in "real time." The interval property is not very accurate.

Label button Tool on the Toolbox that places a Label control on the currently selected form.

Label control Control that is used to display text that can't be directly edited by the user.

LargeChange property The scroll bar property that determines the amount to change the value of a scroll bar when the user clicks the area between a scroll arrow and the scroll box.

lifetime The attribute of a variable determining how long the variable exists in memory. The lifetime of a variable is determined by the method used to declare that variable.

logic error A mistake that causes your program to do something that you didn't intend. Logic errors generally will not stop the program from running. An example of a logic error is using a multiplication symbol in an equation instead of a division symbol: an output of that particular equation would appear as expected but the answer would be incorrect. Also known as a run-time error or bug.

machine language The native language of the computer which consists of numerical codes for each operation. Also known as machine code.

Main window Control center for the Visual Basic IDE, normally located at the top of the screen. The Main window includes the menu bar and tool bar, each which offers the programmer quick and easy access to the various elements of the Visual Basic environment.

MAK file A Project file.

Max property The scroll bar property that determines the maximum value of the scroll bar.

Menu control A control that defines and displays a menu in a Visual Basic program.

Menu design window A tool that makes creating menuing systems quick and easy from within the Visual Basic environment. It is Accessed by pressing the Menu Design Window button on the toolbar or by selecting Menu Design from the Window menu.

method Specific actions done to an object, implemented as if they were built-in procedures. Methods are called, like procedures, by attaching the method name to an object using a convention not unlike object.property.

Min property The scroll bar property that determines the minimum value of the scroll bar.

move method Method used to animate or move controls across the surface of a form.

Name property Property used to define the internal name of a control or form. Names should be descriptive.

object Any element found in a Visual Basic program. Visual objects like command buttons, menus, and text boxes are painted directly on the form to create the user interface for your program. Other objects, like the Timer are not visible to the user.

OPE (Objects-Properties-Events) flowchart A flowchart designed to easily explain the objects in a program and the properties and events associated with those objects. An OPE chart is particularly well-suited for Visual Basic program development.

Option button control Control that exists in a group where only one of the options can be selected at a time. The options are toggled by selecting one of the option buttons. Option buttons look like a small outline circle that, when selected, contains a smaller filled circle. Option buttons are sometimes referred to as radio buttons.

Option Explicit statement Statement used in a code module that ensures that all variables used in a Visual Basic program must be declared before they are used.

P-Code Partially translated code that the Visual Basic compiler creates when an EXE file is generated. The p-code is interpreted by the Visual Basic interpreter as the program is executed. P-code execution is faster than normal source code interpretation, but slower than true compiled EXE files.

painting The act of placing controls on a form, similar to using a paintbrush to place colors on a canvas. The painting of controls on a form's surface is the most important aspect of Visual Basic interface design.

Picture property A property used to determine which graphics picture will be displayed by an Image control by assigning a file name and path.

Proc A shortened form of Procedure.

Procedure A block of code that can be called by name from elsewhere in a program. Procedures are designed to provide a modular and logical grouping of code that needs to be reused over and over in a program.

program A series of instructions that causes the computer to perform certain tasks

programmer Person who writes, or codes, a computer program using a programming language.

programming language A language designed to facilitate the compilation of human-readable source code.

project Logical grouping of source code files, form files and external controls that make up a Visual Basic program.

project file A text file, with a MAK extension that lists the files that define a Visual Basic program. Also called a make file.

Project window The window in the Visual Basic IDE that lists the various files that make up the current project.

properties   Attributes given to controls that allow the Visual Basic programmer to customize each of the objects in a program.

properties window   The window in the Visual Basic IDE where control properties are displayed and manipulated by the programmer. The settings available in the Properties window vary depending on which control or form is selected.

pseudocode   A specific but still English-like description of the steps that a program is to perform when a particular event occurs to a particular object. Programmers use pseudocode to quickly design a rough code outline of a programming project.

Randomize statement   Statement used to initialize the random number generator assuring that subsequent calls to the Rnd function do not return repetitive numbers.

Rem statement   Statement used to add comments remarks or explanatory lines to a Visual Basic programs Rem is short for remark. The apostrophe (ë) character can be used in place of Rem.

reserved word   A word that is part of the Visual Basic language and as such is reserved for use by the system. For example, the words If, Then and Else are reserved words and cannot be used to declare variables or constants, or be used to name forms or controls.

Rnd function   A function that returns a random number between 0 and 1 (for example, 0.545779).

run   The action of carrying out the instructions in a program. Also known as execute.

Run button   The button on the toolbar in the Visual Basic IDE that causes the current project to be executed. Pressing the Run button, which resembles the Play button on a VCR or audio CD player is analogous to pressing F5, or choosing Start from the Run menu.

Save button   Button on the Main window that is used the save the current project, form, and module files. The button resembles a diskette.

scope   An attribute that determines the visibility of a variable. Variables declared within a procedure, for example, are only visible within that procedure. Their scope is that procedure.

scroll arrow   Small arrows found at either end of a scroll bar that can be clicked to facilitate a small change in the scroll barís value.

Scroll Bar   A special type of control that allows the user to easily navigate through a long list of information. Scroll bars can also be used to facilitate user input. There are vertical and horizontal scroll bars.

Scroll Box   A small box found between the scroll arrows on a scroll bar that determines the current value of the scroll bar. Sometimes called the thumb.

Select Case statement   Statement that replaces multiple nested If-Then-Else statements, making a program easier to code, read, and understand. The Select Case statement tests whether an expression falls within a range of values and then executes certain lines of code based on that test.

SetFocus   A method that is used to change the focus in a Visual Basic program.

Settings box   A text edit box at the top of the Properties window that allows the user to enter control property settings.

Shape control   Control that displays simple graphical objects like rectangles, ovals or rounded rectangles directly on a form. These shapes are used primarily in backgrounds because they are not very detailed.

Single   A data type used to store a number that can have digits to the right of the decimal point, like 3.14. Single is short for single-precision floating point number.

SmallChange property   The scroll bar property that determines the amount to change the value of a scroll bar when the user clicks a scroll arrow.

source code   A human-readable program, written by a programmer in a specific programming language.

startup form   The form that first loads when a program is run. By default, programs with only one form use that form as the startup form. If there is more than one form in a program, the programmer can decide which form is used as the startup form.

Static statement   Statement used to declare a variable that needs to retain its value after the procedure it is declared within has ended. The lifetime of a variable declared with Static is the lifetime of the entire program.

String   A data type used to hold a sequence of characters called a string.

subroutine   A Procedure.

syntax error   A grammar error in a source code program that is detected by the compiler. Visual Basic forces the programmer to fix all syntax errors before it will run the program currently being developed. A typical syntax error would be misspelling a keyword: for example, if the word Caption was misspelled as Captain, a syntax error could result.

TabIndex property   Property that determines which control on a form has the initial focus and the order in which the various controls get the focus as it is changed. The term TabIndex refers to the traditional Windows convention of using the Tab key to switch the focus from one control to another.

Text Box control   Control that can display text. Unlike the label control, however, the text in a text box can be changed by the user. Sometimes called an edit box.

Timer control   Control that is used to cause events to occur at specific time intervals. Once a timer is enabled, it sends timer event messages at the specified time intervals.

timer event   An event caused by a timer control.

Timer event procedure An event procedure that is triggered by a Timer event.

titles The main selections in a menu system.

toolbox A floating palette with buttons representing Visual Basic controls. Controls are selected by single-clicking on the appropriate button. That control is then considered active and can be placed on the form window.

Val function A function that returns the numeric value of a string of characters.

Value property Scroll bar property that determines the current position of the scroll box in the scroll bar.

variable A variable holds a value that can be changed while the program is running. Variables have a name, which is the word you use to access the variable in your code, and a data type.

VBRUN300.DLL Dynamic Link Library file that is required for Visual Basic-generated EXE files to execute. VBRUN300.DLL is automatically placed in the WINDOWS\SYSTEM directory when Visual Basic is installed.

VBX (Visual Basic custom control) File that defines a controls that can be included in your program. The tools, or controls, that appear in the Toolbox are VBXs.

Vertical Scroll Bar control The vertical type of scroll bar. See scroll bar.

Index